Thai Odyssey

By

Loretta J. Dunbar

PublishAmerica
Baltimore

© 2007 by Loretta J. Dunbar.
All rights reserved. No part of this book may be reproduced, stored in a retrieval system or transmitted in any form or by any means without the prior written permission of the publishers, except by a reviewer who may quote brief passages in a review to be printed in a newspaper, magazine or journal.

First printing

At the specific preference of the author, PublishAmerica allowed this work to remain exactly as the author intended, verbatim, without editorial input.

ISBN: 1-60441-012-4
PUBLISHED BY PUBLISHAMERICA, LLLP
www.publishamerica.com
Baltimore

Printed in the United States of America

To my friends in Ban Pong and Uthai Thani, Thailand, with grateful thanks

Author's Note

I have served in the United States Peace Corps on three occasions. Each time, I struggled through three months of training before being posted to a village. My first service was in 1971 in a tiny fishing village on the coast of Ghana, formerly known as the Gold Coast of West Africa. At the age of 40, I was older than my fellow volunteers. I was trained to teach office practices, typing and shorthand in a small boarding school in Axim. The grade level was approximately junior high and above. That particular tour was a turning point in my life and is recorded in my autobiography.

My second tour was on the island of Antigua in the Caribbean—again, a tropical climate, much the same as West Africa, but without the lush foliage. My teaching assignment was similar to that in Ghana, and it was at a small junior college. That was 1985 and I was 54 years young and older than most other volunteers in my group.

Once again in 2004 I applied for a third tour and was assigned to Thailand. The following essays were written that year. I was the only Peace Corps volunteer in a town of about twenty thousand people. As such, I was in high demand. But when I wasn't teaching or "on show", I enjoyed as much solitary time as possible. Because the heat was so intense, I did not voluntarily spend time out of doors. It was during those snatches of solitude that I did my writing.

There were so many interesting things happening around me in Thailand, things that most visitors don't have an opportunity to experience, that I felt an urge to share these encounters with the family at home. Thus, the vignettes that follow chronicle my time in Thailand. They also share a glimpse of life in the Peace Corps. I heartily recommend it to you adventurers out there.

A Day in the Life of a Peace Corps Trainee

January 20, 2004—Training Site: Ban Pong, Thailand, approximately 75 kilometers west of Bangkok.
It is six o'clock in the morning and a voice on the loudspeaker begins my day with a recording of "Around the World I Searched For You..." followed by at least an hour of news, read in Thai language. I'm guessing that this public address system is for the benefit of those citizens without access to radio, TV, or newspaper. This is the start to every day—Sunday included. But never mind; birds and chickens had announced dawn around 5 a.m.

I am living with a Thai homestay family comprised of dad, mom, grandmother, four grown children, a spouse and two grandchildren. They are self-employed in farming and trucking. The family is relatively well off. I am lucky—it is a good assignment.

It cooled down into the 70s last night and felt wonderful. As I stretch, I become aware of the hardness of the bed. It is a four-inch thick mattress that is hard as a rock, harder than sleeping on a carpeted floor. The mattress rests on an elevated wooden platform. I was ultimately able to substitute the Peace Corps-issue 'brick' of a pillow with a softer one. Many Thais sleep at floor level. I have no chair. There is a low, square coffee table in my twelve-foot square room. This requires me to sit on the floor to do any writing, homework, etc.

One of the first Thai phrases I learned was *hong nahm yoo tee nai?* Where is the toilet? By and large toilets are Eastern style: a porcelain fixture with molded footprints on either side of a low bowl. One squats and straddles the fixture. It does not flush; instead, one steps off the fixture, scoops a dipper of water from a nearby reservoir and sloshes it into the bowl. No toilet paper; instead one wipes with the left hand, and then there is a hose to finish off; a crude rendition of a bidet. Toilets were one of my first hurdles. There are Western toilets very occasionally, but they often don't have a piped-in water source, so one still must use a dipper for flushing. Few sanitary systems can accommodate toilet paper (which is rarely present anyway), but if you carry your tissue around with you (and I do), there is the dilemma of disposing of the soiled tissue. Some toilets have a bucket for waste paper disposal.

Next is the bathroom. In my present circumstance, there is a tiled room about eight feet square, with a cistern in one corner and piped-in water to keep it filled. In some cases there is a showerhead installed, but in two-story homes there often is insufficient water pressure to service a shower on upper floors. Instead, one uses a plastic scoop to dip into the cistern and slosh the contents over one's body. Yes, it is cold! But it works.

You are now standing in water on a tiled floor that slants to a drain hole. Remember, this is how you shampoo your hair, too. Finally, you dry off and go on with life. It is unseemly for women to show their bare shoulders, so I wrap in a sarong to go to and from the bathroom and drape a towel over my bare shoulders.

Another cultural aspect to adjust to is that of never wearing shoes in the house. Since the kitchen, dining area and shower room are all in separate areas outside of the main house, where the bedrooms are, and with cement floors joining the areas I am forever slipping into plastic flip-flops on the cement areas and then kicking them off to walk barefoot on the beautifully tiled indoor areas.

Housing, in general, is very interesting. Of course, most is very basic. Living, cooking, and socializing are mostly done out of doors, because of the weather. Therefore, not a lot of attention is paid to the inside of the house, excepting in the nicer homes.

For instance the main house where I am staying has beautiful, highly polished hardwood parquet floors, with ceramic tile flooring on verandahs and porches, as well as bathrooms and toilets. There are screens at the windows to keep out the multitude of mosquitoes but that doesn't eliminate other types of insects and geckos. A gecko is a small lizard. Most geckos have no eyelids and instead have a transparent membrane which they lick to clean. Many species have specialized toe pads that enable them to climb smooth vertical surfaces and even cross indoor ceilings with ease. They often make their home inside human habitations and become part of the indoor menagerie. Geckos are seldom really discouraged because they feed on insect pests and can be quite entertaining to watch.

There is adequate electricity and good lighting. Some bedrooms even have individual air-conditioners. However, open-window ventilation is the norm. This allows a lot of dust to filter into every crevice and fold. Indoor housekeeping is not a priority, excepting that floors are kept swept and cleaned. Very little attention is paid to storage. There are no built-in closets. A separate cupboard must be acquired for shelf and hanging storage. It is customary to use a flimsy, free-standing structure about thirty inches wide, with several horizontal bars for hanging and draping clothing—something like a clothes drying rack. Sometimes, clothing is folded in piles until used, and then ironed at the last minute before wearing.

At last, we come to breakfast. I am often served warmed, sweetened soy milk along with a couple of donut-like pastries. Not bad at all. But after I had been living with my Thai family for a short time, I started bringing in yogurt and fruit. At all odds, I want to avoid starting my day with some form of the customary rice soup. I don't care for rice three times a day. I haven't seen a potato since leaving Seattle on January ninth.

Breakfast over with, I brush my teeth, grab my daypack with texts and other items and hop on my bicycle. I generally bike an average of five or six kilometers a day, going to a Wat where I teach English classes in the mornings, and then after lunch, a bike ride to another Wat to attend Thai language classes for about three and a half hours each day. At noon, I meet with a couple of other trainees and have lunch at an outdoor food stand. Bike riding in the heat is challenge enough, but add to that the mangy stray dogs along the way. Only some of them are threatening, but those can be terrifying. Dogs are a primary concern to all volunteers. Buddhism disallows killing anything, so there are millions of dogs in the country that would make the SPCA weep.

People living along my bike route wave, stare, call out and honk. I live completely in a fishbowl. There is nothing I do that is not known by all and sundry. Even across town they know my movements.

Let me mention here that some roads are only one lane wide. There are endless motorcycles and scooters on the road, along with minibuses, bicycles and larger vehicles—all in competition for road space. Driving is on the left, as a rule, but that doesn't prevent drivers from using whatever road space is available, even oncoming lanes.

Peace Corps requires us to be "suitably dressed"—called *rip roy*—whenever out and about, and particularly in the classroom. Thus, each morning I don trousers and a pair of sturdy shoes or sandals to ride the (male) bike to the classroom. When I arrive there, I must then change into a skirt and suitable shoes. The reverse is true when returning home. I leave a skirt and shoes at my teaching school and do a quick change each day. Remember, that we are in scorching heat and humidity all the while.

In the beginning of Thai time, wats were not only religious centers, but sometimes educational and medical centers, thus most schools are a part of a wat compound. The buildings are beautifully ornamented, just as you see in travel brochures, yet chickens and dogs are abundant around the grounds. They must have been hiding during the photo shoots. Wats are as common in Thailand as Baptist churches are in the southern United States.

My day progresses, and now it is supper time. Many households do little cooking; instead, they purchase from the market or street venders. I will discuss the food aspect in a later essay.

I'm at the end of my workday—almost. Having returned safely to my host family home at about 5 p.m., I replenish lost fluids with lots of water, which we carry with us at all times.

THAI ODYSSEY

After several hot, sweaty days, it is time to *sahk pah*—do laundry. Outside, I squat on a low stool near a water tap, and fill a large plastic wash tub with cold water. There is a flat board and a stiff scrub brush near at hand to use for removing the worst soil around collars and elsewhere. A good wash and a couple of rinses and I'm ready to turn everything inside out to prevent sun fading and hang the clothes on galvanized clothes horses. In the morning they will be dry.

Time for bed.

My Thai Family

As a part of our training, we are required to live with a Thai family throughout the training period. The purpose is to introduce us to Thai culture and give us a chance to practice our Thai language skills (and lack thereof). Thai families volunteer their homes for this purpose. I am living with a lovely large family. The eldest is "Ya" (grandmother), who is 79 years old and is the mother of the husband. The husband, Tim Kasaetlaksamee and Kuhn (Mrs.) Kasaetlaksamee have five children: (I'll use their nicknames here—which is standard Thai practice) Song, elder son aged 30, is married to Eed aged 24. They have a daughter, Nayo aged 3 and a son, Name aged 2.

Next in line is Karuna, eldest daughter aged 28, who more or less looks after my well being. She speaks a little English, is a college graduate and works as a lab technician. Then there is a daughter, Pui aged 22, who attends university in Chiang Mai. I haven't met her yet. Second son is Boy aged 21. He is the child who gave up his bedroom room for my nine weeks with them. Last, but not least is Breeze, a sweet-faced 15-year-old who attends a Catholic girl's school.

If you're keeping count, there are eleven of us sharing this home. There are two *hong nahms* in working order and one bathroom. One must carefully and watchfully set out to take a dipper-bath when the room is available. There is a bathroom with a western toilet on the second-floor level where I sleep, but the water pressure can't reach that high, so a lovely tiled shower room goes unused, except for the western toilet. To use that wonderful amenity, I switch on an electric pump that just barely produces enough water pressure to the second floor to provide the luxury of a flushing toilet, but not enough pressure to reach the showerhead.

When I enter the bathroom, I flip on the pump switch. As soon as I flush the toilet, I turn off the pump, because the cistern can't hold water for more than one flush at a time. A western, flushing toilet is a luxury here, but not necessarily coveted by Thai people. The family is fairly well to do. "Pa" owns a trucking business, which Song pretty much manages. The real income is from farming. The house I live in is situated within a walled/fenced yard that is in conjunction with the trucking business. There are massive big trucks in the yard, and other large equipment. The farm production seems to be in plots all around this area.

There are two other homes clustered within a small radius, each one belonging to brothers of my host, and each one fairly well to do. The main house is beautiful—I described it a little in a previous chapter. There is a covered walkway at one side with an adjoining set of bedrooms for the extended family—Song and his wife and family. The kitchen/dining area is alongside these rooms—out in the open. Ma cooks on three coal-fed braziers using woks. There is one gas burner. Very often, as I come down for breakfast, I see her using mortar and pestle.

The funny thing is this is quite a modern home. There is a lovely kitchen that is being used mainly for storage. It seems that the "old ways" suit ma, and she has never attempted to use a modern stove.

We never sit down to a meal all together. People come and go at all times of day and evening and sometimes I sit with two or three family members and at other times I might sit and eat alone—especially at breakfast time. The large, heavy wooden table could probably seat ten people; some of the chairs have missing back supports. Water is piped in at a kitchen sink, cold only—no hot water. Dirty dishes are rinsed and left in the sink until someone decides to wash up. Not many dishes collect before washing up is done by any one of the females in the family.

There is a great variety of food served. However, I begin to notice that what isn't eaten today will be found on the table tomorrow, along with the new dishes of the day. In between meals, the food sits in the middle of the dining table in serving dishes and covered over with a very large, plastic, dome-like protective covering. It is never, repeat, never refrigerated. When you consider the climate, one wonders why we don't get food poisoning. But it works. Milk, yogurt, eggs and water can be found in the fridge, but little else. Rice and noodles are staples. There are many tasty dishes. However, I have become semi-vegetarian. The poultry and meats look fine, but when cleavered into pieces at random, with no regard for bone joints, there are splinters of bone to be found in every mouthful. Right now, there is a major concern about bird flu in this area. Consequently, I occasionally eat pork or beef grilled over hot coals—which is very tasty—with a dish of rice and vegetables. Often, I just eat steamed vegetables and snack on peanuts for protein. I haven't seen a salad since Seattle, but that will come when I have my own abode and can cook "American" once in a while. Fish is served at every meal, but I'm leery of the many bones on the whole fish, head and tail included, and steer clear. Many households regularly send out for food from roadside venders.

I live in a rural area on the outskirts of Ban Pong, surrounded by sugar cane fields. It is generally quiet, except for the blasted P.A. system (close to my bedroom window) that revs up at 6:00 a.m. every day and continues for a couple of hours.

Each day I observe something new in family interaction. They are very spirited, friendly and relaxed. They couldn't be kinder to me, trying to guess what I might like to eat, bringing goodies to the table to see if I accept them and supplying bottled drinking water by the quart bottle six-pack. I truly want for nothing.

Out on the forecourt tonight, there are half a dozen massive baskets overflowing with a small, dark green fruit the size of a lime, called *mankute*. Pretty soon family members sit on squat wooden stools in front of large washtubs filled with water, and begin culling out the bad fruit, washing and counting the good ones, and returning them to those same large baskets, now carefully and skillfully lined with freshly cut banana leaves straight from the trees in the garden. Father and daughter count out 1200 pieces of fruit to each basket. They were quite surprised when I drew up a squat stool and sat to help wash and transfer the fruit from washtub to basket. It is fun to be able to offer some assistance and work alongside the family, despite the fact that there can be no casual conversation among us.

Entrepreneurship abounds in Thailand. Apparently *mankute* are grown on nearby plots of ground. It is sold in the market and is an ingredient used in making shampoo, as well as detergent. Over the course of my stay, we went through this work process several evenings.

Tonight, pa cut down a bunch of bananas from a nearby tree in the yard for us to enjoy. There are other fruit trees around the premises and ma walks out into the yard and plucks greens for some of the dishes she prepares. There is no garden as such, things just grow at random.

Everyone works at something or other, except Ya. She seems not to be quite all there. She more or less wanders around, sometimes talking to herself. But she wears a sweet smile, has a nice bedroom and is well fed and looked after. She has no teeth and appears to be gumming (and spitting) betel nut all day. She is only seven years my senior. That is what fascinates the family about my being here. Having all my own teeth is a source of wonderment. They continue to be amazed that I can ride off on my bike each day and return in the late afternoon after a long, hot day slaving over language textbooks and pupils.

This is my "home away from home" and my Thai family. I believe they are of Chinese descent and that most of our food is more Chinese than Thai. In the beginning, I was rather dreading this homestay experience, but it is turning out to be a treat. The young folks assist me with my Thai language homework most evenings and more or less vie for the privilege. It certainly aids my acquisition of the language—which is the object of the drill—along with cross-cultural exchange.

Bits and Pieces

I had an opportunity to practice Thai language the other day when I found my bike chain had slipped off the sprockets. Language class had finished and I was the last to leave. I had just learned to say "help" in Thai, so now was the time to put it to use. I approached two girl students who were playing ping pong nearby. I excused myself in Thai fashion, and asked for help—*chuay duay*. Happily, they were able, with the aid of a twig, to put the chain back in place.

Here are some of the little things that make up my day.

Those of us who haven't conformed to the Asian squat toilet, i.e. using water to cleanse the derrière in the *hong nahm*, must carry toilet paper with us at all times. In addition, I carry a "hankie" with me to wipe my hands after washing them. Not surprisingly, there are no paper towels. Hankies also substitute for a napkin at mealtime. It is either that or wipe my hands on my clothes.

Remember, I also carry bottled water with me most of the time. Consequently, I can't simply leave the house with only a handbag each day; I must carry a daypack to cart around all personal needs plus school papers, English/Thai dictionary, cell phone (my first ever), snacks, etc. The daypack also acts as a shopping bag for carrying purchases back to the house. Remember, too, that I am traveling by bicycle, *songtao* or on foot.

A *songtao* might be described as a long-bed pick-up truck with a roof and open sides, and with padded bench seats on either side. Sometimes there are canvas or plastic side curtains that can be unrolled and lowered in the event of a sudden shower.

Songtao means "two rows". When I want one to stop and pick me up, I simply stand at the roadside, arm outstretched, palm down, and they stop. When I want to get off, I push a buzzer a few meters from my stop—and the driver stops. It needn't be at a corner; it can be in the middle of a block or at a dusty intersection in the country. The first trick is to decide where the *songtao* goes and on what time schedule. That is easy enough if you know Thai language. On the other hand, most of our local knowledge is gained by constant observation. If a *songtao* passes near my house, I simply monitor its schedule to find out when it passes and at what intervals. When catching a *songtao* from town, I can mention the name of the wat (temple) nearest my home and someone will direct me to the right vehicle at a specified corner in the town. Each route begins and ends on a different corner. I can practically set my watch by the one that runs every thirty minutes past my house. It costs 10 baht each way—about twenty-five cents. Since we Peace Corps folks stand out like a sore thumb in the town, after the first run or two on the *songtao*, the driver knows my stop and I don't need to ring the buzzer, he simply stops at my house. The biggest drawback is that the service stops running at 6 p.m.

For you gals out there, there is no need for makeup. It would melt off before you leave the house. Never have I been so blasé about my appearance. I rarely use moisturizer; the humidity takes care of that. It is not uncommon for Thais to make copious use of talcum powder—male and female—even on the face, but especially on areas of the body that sweat the most. In this humidity, my hair's natural tendency to curl is a boon. Since I wear one of those oh-so-deplorably-ugly helmets whenever on the bicycle, hair style is a thing of the past. I'm about ready to brave a local salon for a haircut.

Dressing up is hopeless. Try being stylish while pedaling a male-type bike, fending off snarling dogs, dodging potholes, wiping sweat from your eyes in 90 degree heat, and wondering who just sent a text message on my cell phone. Most likely it is Seth. He loves those text messages—and I love receiving them. I was running late for language class the other day (daughter Mary had telephoned from Texas just as I was mounting my bike) and Seth texted to ask if I was okay. That is a warm fuzzy feeling. We all tend to look out for one another.

Some of you know that I love orchid plants. They are common here and need little attention. I can't wait to have my own house where I can surround myself with orchids in bloom. And the variety of fruits and vegetables is delightful. I saw great looking asparagus in the market today. No need to want for good food. I perused a couple of small shops and found peanut butter and canned tuna—I long to have my own kitchen. There is a fantastic bakery in town, too. I confess that I'm missing whole-grain products, but I might find some of those in time—especially on rare visits to Bangkok.

I'm not having withdrawal pains yet, but I surely will soon, for I truly miss Mexican food, a staple for me in the States at least once a week. This afternoon, several of us met at a real restaurant, as opposed to a roadside vender, and were able to order a Western-style meal. When I was issued a knife, instead of a tablespoon, along with a fork, I was puzzled about using it. This was the first time my food wasn't served in bite-size portions. There was even a side salad and French fries. Wow—it was a treat.

Let's talk pests (one at a time). We'll start with pesky ants. Tell me, what self-respecting ant would invade my pill box and dine on multivitamins and cod liver oil gelcaps? If I bring a single edible crumb into the room, the ants have at it before I can hang it from the ceiling. In that case, it takes them at least five minutes to find it. I have invested in a couple of plastic food savers, but I've been careless a time or two, and the ants have taken unfair advantage of me.

I love the way we improvise here. Today I changed my bed linens. Forget fitted sheets. We knot each corner of a flat sheet and, *voilà*, a fitted sheet! Part of the fun and the challenge of this adventure is improvisation. There is a great sense of accomplishment when I can fill a need without a local Wal-Mart. Shopping in the hundreds of small kiosks in hidden alleyways is exciting in the extreme. You never know what you'll discover. Beats the heck out of an air-conditioned mall. Just this weekend in a food market, a monster rat crossed our path and scared the begeezuz out of Seth.

LORETTA J. DUNBAR

Just for the record, here are a few current Peace Corps statistics gathered at orientation in Seattle: there are presently 7,000 serving volunteers. The average age is 28, 61% female and 39% male. Our group is lucky; we're 19 women and 17 men—a nice ratio. We like having those guys around. Worldwide, 9% of current volunteers are married, 6% are over 50 and there is one volunteer who is 84 years young. Since its inception in 1961, 169,000 caring folk have served. And it is still "the toughest job you'll ever love." I am the oldest volunteer in Thailand; not sure where I rank internationally, but probably close to the oldest.

Pepsi and Coke vie with each other. Beer is a strong contender; whiskey is less common (too expensive on our modest allowance). We discovered wine coolers at the local 7-11 shop, and I've given those a taste test. We had our first birthday party last week. Derek turned 23. A lot of us gathered at an open-air restaurant (for want of a better description) and honored his special day. Many of us are anxious that we be able to visit our friends once we get to our appointed sites. Friendships and attachments are being made and we are truly becoming "family". In many cases, the distances can be great; visiting a friend could mean an all-night bus ride.

Last night, when two-year-old Name returned from a visit to his other grandma, he ran to me to be held on my lap and cuddled. That is the best time of my day. His little hands reached up to explore my face, tweaking my nose, rubbing under my chin and running his fingers through my wavy, gray hair. I threaten to put him in a suitcase and take him home to South Carolina with me. Thais are not a "touchy, feely" culture so I relish this opportunity to cuddle this little guy, and I know this is possibly an unusual relationship for him. I'm pleased that the family encourages this give-and-take with Name and joins in the laughter when we tease one another. Tonight when he tweaked my nose, I "honked". That set him laughing. I'm now beginning to pick up some of his phrases in Thai. I'm almost up to his level of speech!

A Peek at My Site

Miracles do happen, and I finally made it to midpoint in training. Our progress has been reviewed, and apparently we've all made it this far. Many are better at language than I am. As my instructor says, "There is room for improvement."

On Monday, February 10, our site assignments were revealed. It was exactly one month earlier that we arrived in Bangkok in the middle of the night, bleary-eyed and tired from a very long plane ride.

It has been one busy month. Lots of excitement with the site announcements. My fellow Peace Corps Trainees (PCT) are going to all corners of Thailand. We spent several days learning language appropriate to finding our way to our sites by one means or another for a preview. We are instructed to meet our co-teachers, see the schools, get acquainted with the town, and look at prospective housing—a scary assignment for those of us less gifted with language.

Yesterday was Valentine's Day. I and the family went out in the evening for dinner—ten of us. I brought home a bouquet of roses for the mother of the family the night before. Interestingly enough, the bouquet was placed in a lovely vase with no water (foil wrapping still remaining on the stem ends), and left to die a natural death before the buds could blossom, and where they remain to this day. This is not a matter of neglect, but rather, I think, from not being accustomed to this type of gift. Artificial flowers are more common. Our cultural differences are interesting to observe.

I spent time today reviewing language. I'm packed and ready to go. Seth, along with his host family, is picking me up for a ride to the bus station early tomorrow morning.

LORETTA J. DUNBAR

Saturday, February 21, 2004: Back from a visit to Uthai Thani, my home-to-be for the next two years. Seth and I had no trouble making the bus journey from Ban Pong to Kruen Tep (aka Bangkok), then a taxi from one bus terminal to another, where we found our respective buses leaving north out of Bangkok. Suddenly it was time for me to board a bus for Uthai Thani. Without a 'by your leave', Seth disappeared in a different direction to catch his bus some distance north of my destination. I was left on my own with my insufficient language skills. As in travel abroad in years past, I managed well enough with gestures and sign language. People the world over are wonderful to traveling strangers—many a time I have had sympathetic folks assist me along my journey from point to point.

It had taken just short of four hours to make the journey from Bangkok to Uthai Thani. Upon arrival at the bus station, I telephoned the director of the school and attempted to convey that I had arrived. After my initial rehearsed patter in Thai, I was lost with his response. I handed the phone to my Thai seatmate, who cleared up the situation and I was told that someone was coming for me. She waited with me at the bus station until the brand new Toyota school van appeared twenty minutes later, with a driver and two English-speaking Thai teachers with whom I will be working.

My hostess, and translator, speaks fairly good English, as do several other teachers, I later learned. Kuhn Tim was nearly beside herself with the excitement of my arrival. She had a large red sign with "Welcome Loretta Dunbar to… (and the foot-long names of two schools written in Thai language)". I was presented with "good luck" flowers—a Thai custom that I had experienced on arrival in January. She hosted my stay for three days and nights, at the end of which time she was emotionally and mentally exhausted with the effort of speaking English almost non-stop for that period of time.

Uthai Thani has a population of just over 18,000. The rice fields and clean air are a welcome change from the sugar cane fields and industrial pollution that I left behind in Ban Pong. The province has several sites of interest that I hope to investigate in good time. Being without motorized transportation is a pain. Can't go far afield by *jak a yan*, aka bicycle.

I was introduced to the student body at my first school via telecast, and presented with more flowers and plenty of picture taking. I was able to at least introduce myself in Thai—and that was a stretch. It is quite a nice school, with substantial classrooms, a computer room and Internet connection. The various officials on the Board of Education of the two schools I will serve were overwhelming in their kindness and hospitality. They treated me like a VIP and seem very pleased and anxious for me to join them in just less than a month.

I was also introduced to the community at large at a town council meeting, who were instructed to look after me and keep me safe. A really warm setting.

Then there was the job of finding a house to live in. Needless to say, not an easy task. I declined everything I saw the first day, but on day two we discovered, via the grapevine, a tiny 'townhouse' on the outskirts of town, where it should be quiet, with any luck. It is probably thirty feet wide by sixty feet long: a living/dining area, one reasonable size bedroom and another tiny bedroom, a miniscule bathroom with western flushing toilet (amen) and the inevitable cistern with dipper for bathing. However, there is a shower attachment on the wall. I'm disenchanted with wet bathroom floors altogether, but it is a way of life.

Peace Corps is obsessed with our safety and houses must meet pretty stiff criteria: fencing, barred windows, sturdy locks, screens, and the list goes on. My primary attraction to this tiny abode is that it is brand new, never before lived in. I negotiated with the friendly landlady for several items. She offered to rent it fully furnished and all utilities (no phone line available). However, I reasoned that in that case, I would need to accept her choice of furniture, and that didn't suit me. The place requires small-scale furniture and I was afraid I'd come into a three-piece overstuffed living room suite that took up the entire space. Or worse still, used cast-off furnishings with suspect cleanliness.

I asked her to put an air-conditioner in my bedroom in lieu of furniture for the house. (Remember, all of this negotiating is being translated both ways through a third person.) I reasoned that if, in the future, I need to move house, at least I'd have furniture. I asked for all kitchen appliances, plus an electric teapot and a fan. I agreed to pay the electric bill over and above the normal allowance, due to the added air-conditioner. All this for just under $95 a month.

Lest you think I made a good bargain, many Peace Corps trainees were gifted with large, fully furnished homes that look like palaces next to mine, plus all modern conveniences—for the same cost. On the other hand, one guy found only a fourteen-foot square tin roofed hut and no running water in his tiny village—also for the same price. We run the gamut on housing; it pretty much depends upon the location and size of the town you are sent to.

My house is a four-plex on a rough dirt road. There are two windows in front and one at the back (I have shared inside walls on either side). I am worried about lack of adequate cross breeze and fear that I might swelter most of the year. Time will tell. The newness was a big selling point with me. I'll have at least three kilometers to bike to school in town, and then back. When I audibly pondered what I'd do in the rainy season, the principal said she would send a school van for me. I think they'll do everything they can to see me safe and comfortable.

I won't be going out after dark on the bike, so any social life will be with co-workers who have cars. I am specifically forbidden to ride a motorcycle even as a passenger—if caught doing so, it is grounds for immediate dismissal from the Corps. To think that I was encouraged to own a motorcycle in Ghana in 1971 during my first tour with Peace Corps! The events of Nine-Eleven and worldwide terrorism have changed Peace Corps regulations dramatically—to the point of intrusion.

More Observations

On day two of my visit to Uthai Thani, I opened the requisite bank account so that Peace Corps can deposit my monthly allowance. I even have an ATM card for cash withdrawals. The allowance will amount to about $175 a month. It was $120 a month in Ghana 31 years ago. House rent is covered separately from this allowance, so we have plenty of money for food, transportation and miscellaneous expenses (or so one is led to believe).

Thai bathrooms are often fully tiled to the ceiling. The toilet, if in the same room, is located pretty close to the hand-held shower or dipper cistern. There is no separate stall. One sloshes water everywhere when bathing with a dipper, and since most toilets are dipper flushed, too, there is often water all over the floor. Of course, if you're going around barefoot, this doesn't matter. You just wipe your feet on the floor cloth (sometimes just an old piece of discarded clothing) placed outside the bathroom door. That is your customary *hong nahm*. Definitely not my favorite room.

There was no public address system to waken me at Kuhn Tim's house where I stayed, but there was a karaoke night spot not far off that played into the wee hours of the morning. Noise pollution is a major hazard. Frequent events are conducted at the site of wat compounds: celebrations of all description. Right now I'm hearing the music and singing of a wedding party through loudspeakers from the wat around the corner here in Ban Pong. With our open-air life style it is next to impossible to lead a quiet existence.

When it came time to depart Uthai Thani for the return to Bangkok and a day-long meeting at Peace Corps headquarters there, six school officials accompanied me to the van park. I opted to return to Bangkok by minivan in order to compare it with the bus service. At the van stop I was presented with a lovely Thai silk sash as a souvenir of my visit. They also purchased the two front seats next to the driver for me, so that I would have plenty of personal space. I left on a happy note and anxious to return and get to work.

Meanwhile, back at the training center, language lessons and classes on teaching skills continue endlessly.

The temperature has climbed and it is very hot by 9 a.m., though between 2 a.m. and 6 a.m. it isn't bad. Ma is always up early preparing breakfast for pa. One day I found her sitting on a squat stool fitted with a serrated blade attached at one end. She was scraping out the inside of a coconut for use in cooking. Earlier, I had seen her walk over to a pile of coconuts, use a sharp tool to remove the outer husk and then whack off the top of the coconut with a machete and take it to the kitchen. The dry outer husk was used as a starter for the coal fire.

This property has an abundance of fruit trees: mangos, pomelo (like a large grapefruit), papaya, bananas and countless other trees and plants that don't exist in the States. Ma often steps into the yard and cuts wild onions and other seasoning grasses to put in the pot.

Maybe this would be a good time to describe the yard around the house. All our meals are eaten under a shelter outdoors. In the evening, it is a constant battle with gnats, mosquitoes flying insects that are attracted to the overhead fluorescent light, and the never-ending pesky ants. If one wants to discard a piece of bone or gristle, it is simply tossed over the short wall into the yard. But that is not the half of it. If I stand at the 'kitchen' sink and look outward, there are beautiful wild flowers of light blue, deep purple and delicate pink amidst egg shells, plastic bottle tops and general debris. The entire property is strewn with plastic bottles, boxes, food containers and all manner of litter—a pile here and a pile there.

Yet the floors and driveway are swept every morning and kept free of debris. Foodstuffs in plastic bags hang from nails here and there.

THAI ODYSSEY

There is a thick layer of dust over anything that doesn't get daily use. There is a permanent patina of grime over the dining table top. It doesn't pay to be finicky. Dust permeates everything. The standard tissue in use is toilet paper. Special plastic containers are made for the roll and it is kept on most dining tables to be used as napkins, nose-blowers, or any other needs.

On the other hand, there is a brightly painted shrine in the front yard that stands about fourteen feet high and is a mini replica of a temple. On specific holidays the family places incense, flowers, food and drink at the shrine. This is a world of contrasts.

These descriptions do not cast aspersions on the wonderfully kind family I live with. These conditions are a way of life in many, if not most homes. Granted, this is a farming family and they are far too busy to be bothered with small niceties. On the other hand, the youngest daughter attends a Catholic school, the next one attends university and the oldest one is educated and has a good job. Domestic standards are simply different from ours in the United States.

Another domestic observation: There are few soft furnishings in the houses. Floors are tile or hardwood and furniture is normally a heavy wooden variety without cushions or upholstery. Thus, every sound echoes; voices are strident and boisterous, so that sound pollution can be deafening. Normal conversation is in loud sharp tones—almost like shouting at times.

A couple of times on a Sunday morning there have been sounds of drumming and dancing in the distance. It grows louder as it nears my room. It turns out to be well-wishers escorting a young monk to his ordination at a nearby wat. And, of course, the early morning P.A. system still wakens us at 6:00, even on Sundays.

Asparagus

Peace Corps devises all manner of extra projects to expose us to Thai culture. This week we were asked to choose a program of interest from a selection of about ten possibilities, which included national games, cooking, dance, etc. I chose to interview an asparagus farmer. It may seem like a strange choice; in fact, I was the only one to make that choice. But I'm fond of asparagus and what better way to learn about it than from a farmer. Add to that, I like doing projects *kuhn dee-oh*—alone—less confusion and more knowledge gathered. I was accompanied by a Thai teacher who interpreted while I interviewed the farmer.

It was a good exercise, and I learned a lot—mostly why asparagus cost so much in U.S. markets. The young farmer was working a plot about a half acre in size. The fern-like plants stand around five feet high in long rows, supported by string stretched between bamboo poles on either side to support these delicate plants. I learned that asparagus can be grown year around and that it takes about seven months from seed to market.

Once a stalk breaks ground, it grows about three inches every twenty-four hours. The interesting thing is that each and every stalk must wear a tiny conical plastic cap by the time it is four inches high. Imagine the labor there. The cap can only be used twice, because the sun causes it to become opaque by that time. If the sun cannot get through, it reduces the value of the product. The cap serves three purposes: it keeps the tip from blossoming, it gives the tip a sharp point and it keeps the stalk green in color. It would otherwise turn white.

While traveling in France a few years ago, I encountered wonderful plump white asparagus at bargain prices. Makes me curious about the process of growing that product.

If I still have your attention, more interesting than the growing cycle of asparagus was the insight to the cooperation of the extended family and the division of labor.

We arrived at the family small holding outside a village just after 8 a.m. Everyone was hard at work, before the blistering sun took its toll. Grandma was gathering bundles of asparagus stalks into wooden containers made to measure each stalk to about ten inches in length. The root ends were cut off and the cut stalks placed on a woven mat for sizing and quality control. Old grandpa was bringing bundles of asparagus from beside the field to the measuring site. Auntie was the quality controller and acting baby-sitter. Somewhere among the rows of asparagus plants were unseen workers stooping and placing caps on spears or pulling up stalks ready for harvest. When the morning harvest ended, all went back to domestic duties.

Auntie was manning a table of bunched asparagus spears for sale at the roadside. She was babysitting the farmer's year-old daughter (her niece), who was being rhythmically rocked by very old grandpa (probably younger than I!) pulling a rope attached to the store-bought cradle that was hanging from bamboo rafters. The lean-to had a corrugated metal roof supported by bamboo poles. The floor was hard-packed gray earth. Auntie sat on a raised wooden platform about the size of a double bed—which is what it was at night. There was a thin mattress covering the platform. A couple more platforms, similar but smaller, served as a play table and a work table (without soft coverings).

This appeared to be Auntie's permanent home. There was a net sleeping hammock hanging at one side, and a smaller hammock used for storage was suspended overhead in the middle of the 'room'. There was a plastic basket with baby toys and a few clothes on hangers hung along the horizontal bamboo support poles.

Meanwhile, grandma is feeding another toddler belonging to a neighbor.

I pondered my reaction, should I be left at this roadside lean-to and told to live in auntie's flip-flops for two weeks.

THAI ODYSSEY

With that thought in mind, I surveyed the rest of the compound. There was one large adjacent building of patchwork corrugated iron, plastic sheets and mats thrown over the roof, and several smaller lean-tos of similar design but made of cardboard or other scavenged materials. Outdoor cookers were made from discarded metal drums. In the midst of this, there is electricity operating a fan and a clock.

Rags, potted plants, tin tubs, defunct motors, cardboard boxes, smaller lean-tos, cages, tires, brooms, bikes, tin cans and never ending plastic bags litter the landscape. In the distance I see a cow, ducks and pigs. I spy a fishing pole in the rafters. There are garments hanging from a bamboo clothes drier and garbage burning nearby. By now, old grandma is sitting on the ground—legs outstretched—working at counting and bundling bamboo sticks (skewers) for fish balls. An unidentified family member sits working with fruit.

Plastic bags storing food, medicines and miscellaneous items hang from any and every protrusion. Canvas half-shades droop limply at the four sides of the primary lean-to, to be available against rain, sun and nightfall. Mangy dogs lie in shade about the grounds. Life seems very helter-skelter, and yet each member of the extended family performs an important role in this ever turning wheel of life.

It is now nearly noon and a beautiful young woman emerges from the field of asparagus to claim her pretty baby daughter. I learned that the young farmer and his wife and baby live nearby—one presumes in better circumstances, judging by dress and a new motorcycle. Still the family works as a unit, with each member contributing for the good of all.

The beautiful asparagus from this plot is destined for the Japanese market. An annual contract keeps the price at a stable level, the farmer has a ready wholesaler and the income appears to be good.

While I sat taking notes, a couple of venders stopped at the compound. In my imagination, I named the first one a "Talat on Wheels". Talat means "market". This was a man driving a motorcycle laden with all manner of fresh vegetables hanging in plastic bags from a metal framework surrounding the cycle. The next vender I called a "Talat on Legs". He was carrying a great bundle of colorful reed mats for sale. You have to admire their efforts at earning a livelihood.

There is a reasonably good "bakery" just up the road where a woman recycles cardboard fashioned into small boxes in which to package her goods. These industrious entrepreneurs serve a purpose in these outlying areas and have a ready market.

There goes a monk on a bike, his orange garment billowing; and a family of four on a motorcycle—a small child wearing a wooly stocking cap and the temperature is in the nineties.

As the months pass by, my essays will dwindle, for my eyes will become accustomed to these strange and wondrous sights. What a pity.

And I still wonder—could I live in Auntie's flip-flops for two weeks and remain unchanged?

Farewell to Wat Ladbourkao

Training is coming to an end and it is time to say goodbye to my first Thai friends. I had the good fortune to have Kuhn Angkana as a co-teacher in this phase of our training program. As I learned new teaching practices, I shared them with my co-teacher and together we worked out lesson plans. I was placed in a particularly supportive school at Wat Ladbourkao and enjoyed a happy practice-teaching experience there. I also believe that I learned as much from Angkana as she learned from me.

A brief description of a school classroom is in order here. The school is fairly old and the rooms are open air. Desks are a bit rickety in some rooms and at the primary level are very basic wooden desks with a storage shelf beneath the desktop.

Children have been learning by rote forever, and the Thai government has embarked on a plan to make education more student-centered and less "teacher talk". It is a difficult concept to switch over to, and that is one of the reasons Peace Corps is here. Thai students can often read and write in English, but are unable to speak it. Not unusual—I'm the same way in a foreign language. It needs constant speaking practice and there just aren't enough native English-speaking teachers in the school system. We are here to help improve the spoken language.

Unfortunately, Thai education offices often don't take into account a teacher's major when assigning positions. My principal had a certificate to teach math, and ended up teaching English for twelve years before becoming principal. He still can't speak English beyond some set phrases. Another teacher studied English, but is assigned to teach math. Go figure.

When I enter the classroom, all students rise and say, "Good morning, teacher, how are you?" in a very sing-song voice. I reply, "Fine, thank you. How are you?" It is no good trying to change the pattern, for they don't really understand what they are saying. We have a mighty job cut out for us, and I feel it will take twice as long as the goal set by the Thai government. But we're here to give it our best.

It should be noted that students have assigned tasks to perform at school, i.e., they sweep classrooms and outside walkways. They are given all kinds of responsibilities. Too, they are often expected to sit in the classroom doing assigned lessons without supervision, while teachers perform other tasks, sometimes administrative, sometimes making paper flowers for a special 'event'. The students are quite accustomed to this unsupervised schooling and some even do well at it.

Ideally, the English teacher should have a room of her own where students can come to her, but this is not an ideal world, and most English teachers are forced to carry their teaching materials with them from classroom to classroom and are teaching English at many, if not all levels. Written English begins in the third grade.

Along with our teaching responsibilities, Peace Corps directs us to embark on a Community Project during the course of this brief training period. This amounts to talking with people in the Thai community in which we live and identifying something that the community wants and is willing to go to some effort to achieve. As a Trainee, I am to be the facilitator only, and the community would produce the end results.

I asked my co-teacher, Angkana, if there were something we might do connected with the school. She conferred with the faculty and quickly replied that they would like to see new landscaping around the base of the flagpole. This is a focal point at the start of every school day, as students and faculty face the flagpole during the raising of the flag, and sing the national anthem.

I took some "before" pictures of the ragged and aged shrubs currently in place at the base of the flagpole. Angkana enlisted the aid

THAI ODYSSEY

of the agricultural teacher, and we were off and running. There wasn't time to embark on a fund-raising scheme for the project, so I and Angkana donated small funds for new plants, and new top soil was donated at a greatly reduced price by the father of one of the students. The student body would provide the labor—even the third graders.

Throughout our two years of service, we are encouraged to do Community Projects at our postings. This is to be a practice run. We only had about five weeks to completion. The project became expanded when the faculty hoped to see new sod around the cement map of Thailand that rests to the left of the flagpole. Then, repainting the map sounded like a good idea. Whoa! Is this getting out of hand?

Not to worry. Every few days I would see changes and improvements, which I dutifully recorded with photographs. Old plants were removed, new soil evenly spread and new plants purchased. I didn't dare to hope to see the end results, but the staff was anxious to have it completed before my departure. I suggested that painting the map could be phase two after my departure.

What a thrill to arrive at the school the last day to find everything completed and the map painted in vivid green and yellow (paint still wet!). I was deeply moved by their efforts to please me.

And then the show began. Students had been taught a couple of short songs of praise and goodbye; some students performed Thai dances, and little ones presented me with long-stem roses, as heart-shaped signs were displayed. It was a good excuse for a party—better known as *sanook*, aka fun—something the Thai people are very good at.

A bountiful lunch was served under the trees on the school grounds and I was presented with a beautiful hand-painted urn in a glass display case. Other small gifts were offered by various faculty members. It is really difficult, if not impossible, to repay these generous people. This is a most warm and thoughtful culture.

As an aside, one of the Thai faculty asked if he could read my palm. He said I would lead a long and healthy life. I responded that I had already done that. He said, yes, but, "you will live to be at least ninety". I've been told this before, and at this age, I'm beginning to believe it. A fellow trainee stood nearby and offered his hand, but the man just shook his head and uttered *nit noy*. This means "just a little". I looked at the trainee's hand and read very short life-lines compared to my own. Eerie.

Tomorrow I will stand before my fellow Peace Corps Trainees and proudly give a five-minute presentation of my Community Project, with a display of "before—during—and after" photographs. What seemed an insurmountable assignment in the beginning has a happy ending.

Now my task is to fill the remaining eighteen years of my 'long' life with fruitful and rewarding activity.

Making a Start in Uthai Thani

Well, I made it. I was sworn in last week and am now a Peace Corps Volunteer for the third time.

During the last week of training, we had a big "thank you" party for our homestay families and performed dancing and singing for them, along with thank-you speeches and dinner. I participated in the Bamboo Dance routine—decked out in Thai dress and heavy makeup. None of us remembered the dance steps correctly, so we faked it. We were so brightly dressed that I figured the audience was too entranced with the costumes to realize that we were dancing out of step.

It was a busy week. The supervisor and a co-teacher from one of my schools in Uthai Thani attended a two-day seminar held prior to the swearing-in ceremony at our training site. That gave us a chance to get better acquainted. Immediately after my swearing-in they put all my baggage in the school van and took me back to Uthai Thani with them (about a three-and-a-half-hour drive), where I spent the first night with my co-teacher, Kuhn Tim. The polite title "Kuhn" is used before the personal name to address both males and females of similar or higher status.

The small town of Uthai Thani is about 235 kilometers north of Bangkok. The topography is generally flat; good terrain for bicycling.

The very next day, we obtained the house key from my landlady and went shopping. I bought a single bed, mattress, clothes wardrobe, kitchen cupboard, a couple of plastic chairs and some incidental house wares. Everything was delivered to the house within the hour; I unpacked sheets and moved in immediately. The landlady did install an air-conditioner in my bedroom, as requested when I negotiated for the house, and that is my salvation. Some of the other promised appliances are second-hand, but usable enough. That is one of the reasons I bargained for a new air-conditioner rather than a fully-furnished house. I want to select furniture to my own taste. There is no back door to the house, no alternative exit, to my dismay. And as I am mildly claustrophobic, this is a source of discomfort. My back wall faces the back wall of a neighboring house and our louvered kitchen windows face each other. There are only two feet separating the two houses and there is an open sewer drainage ditch running through that two-foot space. I had allowed the primary selling points of the house: "small, new and clean", to influence my decision to rent. Alternative choices had been large, old, musty, and sometimes decrepit.

So far, I'm coping just fine, but I can hear, smell and see my neighbors whenever we're in our respective kitchens at the same time. It is not ideal living, but when I bike down the street on the way to town, I realize that I live in pure luxury compared to many along the way. I use the air-conditioner sparingly and generally rely on oscillating fans. I'm waiting to see my first electric bill before spoiling myself with air-conditioning.

My teaching assignment encompasses two grade schools. The respective principals of the schools are a married couple. They are truly dedicated professional educators and were immediately very supportive of me.

The principals have decided that I need to be transported to my respective schools by van every day this first week, until I get oriented. I work two days at one school and two days at the other school. On Fridays I do paperwork and anything required relating to a yet-to-be designated community project. It is only about two kilometers by bike from my home to either school.

Classes are letting out this week for their summer holidays from the end of March to the middle of May, during this extremely hot season of the year. This gives me a lot more downtime than I want, and Peace Corps forbids us to travel away from our site during the first ninety days! I suggest this is extremely bad timing by Peace Corps. The training months were intense and demanding. Now, suddenly, I am in limbo for six weeks, before classes begin next semester.

My new Thai teacher friends are very social and caring folks and they often want to have me out in the evenings. I'm sure my novelty will wear off sooner or later.

I'm frequently approached by people asking me to help them with English. I do plan to teach adult classes to teachers at the schools when the new term begins, however I had to decline categorically, stating that I'm not at liberty to teach privately outside of my Peace Corps assignments. During training, Peace Corps warned us of this eventuality and suggested that if we allowed ourselves to take on all demands on our free time, we'd have absolutely no personal time, and burnout would be inevitable.

So far, my life style is a few steps up from camping out. While the house is new and looks presentable from the outside, plumbing is basic and electrical outlets scarce. Bugs are attracted to the overhead fluorescent strip lights at night, which means that I must sweep out dead gnats, mosquitoes and other beasties each morning. The bathroom is mini size and windowless, and after each shower I must swab the deck with a wet mop kept close at hand, or I would slosh around in bath water.

There is no separate shower stall; there is simply a hand-held showerhead mounted on a wall bracket right next to the western flushing toilet. Cold water only, of course, but in fact it is too warm in this summer heat; it will be too cold in winter, even if the temperature is in the 80s. Construction is not exactly square, so there are gaps around the front door where bugs have easy access. There are screens at the windows, but gnats make it through with ease. Right now we're having four-shower weather—that is, I shower at least four times a day to cool off.

I had no break between swearing-in on Friday and classes on Monday. I was put into the classroom immediately—mainly because the students were so eager to see and hear me. This is actually final exam week and no new material is being taught before their summer break.

I had official introductions at both schools; big excitement all around. Celebrity for a day. School officials couldn't be nicer. If I even mention a need, they offer to fill it. The beautiful director at school number one (they are called 'director' rather than 'principal') presented me with a brand new lady's bike, so that I could wear a skirt to work and not have to change clothes all the time as I did with the Peace Corps-issued men's bike (which I still have). Her husband is director at school number two and he sent over a bigger and better fan for the house and arranged for me to have a desk and chair sent from the district education office. The furniture quality makes Wal-Mart furnishings look posh, but I'm grateful for the workspace and his thoughtfulness. Until the desk appeared, I was bringing my meals to the bedroom on a tray and sitting on a plastic lawn chair to eat.

On Sunday afternoon, I walked into town (I hadn't received the bike yet) to scope the area and get familiar with the route. It must have been near 100°F and I thought I'd melt. That evening when Kuhn Tim came to take me to the Night Market, she arrived in her sister's pick-up truck, accompanied by four motorcycles laden with passengers who wanted to meet me and see my house. Not a stick of furniture in the living/dining area; ten guests; only four water tumblers (I couldn't even offer the customary cold water); only a rinky-dink fan (from landlady) and it must have been at least 95°F or more in the house. We all sat on the cool, blue tile floor, Thai style, and chatted!

I had no intention of mentioning my long walk into town earlier in the day; however, one of the visiting neighbor ladies was quick to tell Tim that she had seen me that afternoon in town. There are absolutely no secrets in this society. What they don't know, they do not hesitate to ask outright. I am made aware that learning Thai language is essential if I'm to get the most from this tour. I truly want to get on with it and have asked everyone to help me on a daily basis, so we exchange English and Thai words and phrases at lunch and any other social time.

Yesterday afternoon one of the new friends who had popped in and had sat on the floor that first evening, brought to the house a dining table and four chairs provided again by the district education office. The table was assembled in the workshop and the top appears to be made of white dry-erase board. The frame is of black, square metal tubing. The chairs are well-used folding chairs from storage and have seen better days. Never mind, now I have a place to eat and a work table to use. I tossed a piece of local cloth over the top and it serves the purpose. So much for selecting furnishings of my own choosing; eclectic in the extreme, but it sure saves money.

I don't know from minute to minute what will happen next. Schedules change frequently; an errand for me might end up three errands for others along the way. It is a great life and I'm still Superwoman in their eyes. They find it hard to believe that I am so "strong", as they put it—which translates into "healthy". I'm being introduced to everybody who is anybody. I've learned to lock my house door when I'm home, because people sometimes just show up and walk in. No doorbells. In this heat I go around half dressed much of the time, so I've learned my lesson.

Challenges are met and conquered daily. Life isn't easy, but it certainly is never dull.

Miscellaneous Observations

Food: There is an abundance of fruit and vegetables in Thailand, and I've learned to enjoy and appreciate much of what is available. Steamed rice is the obvious staple and is consumed three times a day. The proper way to eat it is to take a large spoon of rice on your plate and then help yourself to very small portions (bite-size) from the array of dishes on offer. One eats with a spoon in the right hand and a fork in the left. No knives. Consequently, food is usually cut into bite sizes before cooking. There is almost always a variety of fish—sometimes prepared whole and grilled with head and tail intact. Another time it is prepared in a broth and served over a brazier. Because I am sensitive to fish bone (from a childhood incident), I seldom eat the fish offerings. This entire region is a fish-based economy, so it is sometimes awkward.

Prawns and shrimp are very common. Unfortunately, they too are often cooked with heads and tails—even when battered and deep fried. Very tiny, almost miniscule, shrimp are a favorite flavoring and are found in everything—and eaten whole, shell and all. Grilled pork, beef and chicken are staples. One of my favorite meals is one of these meats very thinly sliced and threaded onto bamboo skewers and grilled over coals and served with peanut sauce—*satay*. I also enjoy stir-fried vegetables as well as fried rice.

A close second staple is noodles in great variety. There are always vegetables and usually a soup offered at mealtime, too. I don't eat spicy food, so I must always ask before I sample a new dish. If it has a red color, it is usually hot. My friends know that I eat *mai pet*—'not hot' food, and that I eat *nit noi*—'small' portions. I do try most everything except *pet*, but one bite is often sufficient to make a negative decision on "seconds". As a guest and an elder, it is common for my host to place portions of food on my plate for me (whether I want it or not). I am gradually training folks to my tastes and portions. When I lived with my Thai family in training, it was wonderful to observe their eating habits. It was common for siblings and parents to share the same drink, use the same straw, taste from one another's plates, etc. Absolutely everything is shared. We could take a lesson in family togetherness. Of course, it is all at the cost of independence. These cultural observations and exchanges are part of the challenges in Thailand. Peace Corps is not for sissies.

Size and scale: Many things are scaled to the petite Thai stature. The door to my bathroom is so low that I just make it through without stooping. Thai-made clothing is difficult for an American to buy. Size XL is still snug on me (I wear an 8 in USA). Shopping is easier in Bangkok, but you are buying imported brands at import prices—no bargains. Shop aisles are narrow; everything is closely packed, allowing access to only slim bodies.

Schools: This is an open-air society. Dust abounds as breezes pass through louvered windows; birds fly in and out of classrooms. Children arrive before 8 a.m. to perform cleaning tasks and other assigned chores. Teachers often must clean their own rooms. Each morning there is a ceremonial raising of the flag and singing of the national anthem. This is followed by five minutes of calisthenics and announcements.

Lunch is offered to students and teaching staff. Tin plates and utensils are provided and everyone cleans up after himself. Teachers are generally smartly dressed, often in long-sleeved jackets. I am sweltering in a short-sleeve cotton blouse. I don't think I can live long enough to get accustomed to wearing heavy clothes in this climate. Shoes are another matter. Smart sandals are often seen, however, slip-on shoes are the most practical, as we leave our shoes at the door in many cases. I personally do not enjoy going barefoot.

THAI ODYSSEY

Uthai Thani has many narrow side lanes and it will take weeks to explore them. I'm first getting used to the main roads and learning my route to the two schools I will serve. Litter is not as bad in Uthai Thani as it was in Ban Pong and I haven't seen as many mangy dogs. There are motorized tuk-tuks and I may employ one once in a while if bicycling becomes tedious, or when I have over-sized packages to take home. My co-teachers are showing me where to find things in the maze of tiny shops around the town.

A visit to Bangkok is another story. Many people wear surgical masks against the pollution. Taxis are cheap and plentiful; most are freshly painted, but on closer inspection they might be ancient and pretty tatty inside. There is little trunk space for luggage. On the bright side, almost anything is available in Bangkok. You just need to know where to find it—no small task. I have yet to explore the city and I'm in no hurry.

Japanese cars are plentiful as well as Fords. Driving is on the left and Thai/English road signs are good in cities and on main highways. Mars Bar, Kit-Kat and Oreo cookies are easy to come by, and there is a KFC and a McDonald's in every major town (not in Uthai Thani). There are Seven-Elevens even in small towns and they are wonderfully handy.

There are quite a number of international volunteer organizations who do work in Thailand. I had occasion to meet a group from Scotland who were here for two weeks to teach English. They were intelligent professionals seeking some cultural exchange while doing a good deed.

Peace Corps encourages us to hold two-day English Camps frequently. I participated in one during training. Normally a school will decide on a need and invite volunteers to participate and help teach. The school provides room and board. Many volunteers do this, and it gives them an opportunity to travel to different areas of the country and experience diverse culture and ecology. The biggest problem is transportation. Many sites are difficult to get to for such short visits.

LORETTA J. DUNBAR

Cell phones are common. I delayed buying one while in training, but finally realized it was a necessity. I haven't used one in the States, so it was a new experience. Here they say, "burr me". The "burr" comes from the word "number", so this means, "call me."
Non-Thai people are called "farang". I just learned the origin of this word. The early European settlers/visitors to the country were from France. "France" became garbled into farang and is an adopted word for all foreign-looking residents or visitors. It doesn't have a negative connotation.

Pomp and Circumstance

Graduation time. It is a festival of color. The stage is festooned in garlands and sprays of fresh flowers hand crafted by my co-teacher, Jirapa. To the right on the stage is a raised platform for a presiding Buddhist monk. Teachers and dignitaries are dressed in bright silk suits or dresses. But the cutest of all are the youngest children in their "cap and gown" outfits.

Final exams are over and it is time to present certificates of completion to students graduating to the next level. We are in a school gymnasium. Parents and families sit along the side, where we would expect to find bleachers, and hundreds of students sit on folding chairs facing the stage. The building is made of grey, unpainted cement breeze blocks and is two stories high. Birds fly in and out of the rafters from time to time. It is only 9 a.m., but already it is too hot for comfort. Industrial floor fans are doing their usual job of rearranging hair styles and creating airborne debris.

I biked to the campus and was ushered to the guest-of-honor area to sit with Kuhn Somlak, the very beautiful and stylish director at one of my teaching schools. Presently, Tan Suchat, the presiding monk, has come to sit among us. To my eyes, he has the look of a classic monk. He is tall, thin and slightly gaunt, with beautifully chiseled facial features as if carved from weathered teak. His hair is clipped to half an inch, he is draped in customary saffron cloth and wearing flip-flops. He greets me with a beatific smile and proceeds to speak in English, to my relief. He invites me to practice the technique of meditation with him some day at the temple. The biggest problem I would have is to sit on the floor, cross-legged Thai style, as they do. It is amazing to see people of all ages sitting comfortably on their haunches for time on end, or with crossed legs or legs curled to one side. These old American legs of mine aren't quite so flexible and tolerant.

But let's get back to the students. The kindergarteners are wearing electric blue gowns and steal the show for "cute". When school begins in mid-May, they will be in first grade. Each succeeding grade level is wearing gowns of distinguishing colors to separate the grades through the primary levels. All are wearing black caps. On close inspection, the caps are made of black, heavy-duty poster board stapled and taped together, along with a gold tassel dangling from a hole punched in one corner.

The leading board of education dignitary sits at a table laden with certificates to be handed out. Monk Suchat takes his platform position with the aid of an assistant. There is a large metal bowl of water on his left side and he holds a cluster of green boughs in his left hand. With these, he will bless each student as s/he passes before him. He dips the tips of the boughs in the water and shakes it over the head of the student.

I should explain here about the customary "wai". The "wai" is a gesture, or posture, Thais use when they greet one other, or to say goodbye and to say thank you. It requires putting both hands together in a prayer-like position at chest level and lowering your head so that the tips of your fingers reach your nose. The specifics about when to "wai" and where to place your hands depend on whom you are "wai-ing". The depth of the bow and curtsy depend on the importance and station of the person being greeted. This greeting replaces our American handshake. Since it requires both hands, I am often caught off guard with items in my hands when I should perform a wai. On an ordinary day, we wai everyone the first time we see them in the day. For instance, I wai every teacher in the school yard each morning the first time I see them. It is a charming custom that quickly feels natural.

Assisted by a teacher, a tiny pre-K "graduate" climbs the stairs to the stage and wais before the lovely board of education representative handing out the certificates, and then walks to the monk and wais again and is blessed. S/he then walks off the stage and takes a seat. It all sounds very orderly, but in reality, kids end up scampering around the floor, getting something to drink, talking with others, and generally having a good time. All the while, there is an ongoing procession of students on stage receiving certificates.

The students in upper grade levels are dressed in customary school uniform: girls in white middy blouses and navy pleated skirts; boys in khaki shorts and white shirts. They come in all shapes and sizes; some petite and beautiful as dolls. Many Thais are of Chinese ancestry and they tend to be less petite than the Thais without mixed heritage.

Last week I attended an end-of-term song and dance performance at a private school. Every student wore Thai dress and performed in one way or another. Most wore stage makeup and some of the girls were positively gorgeous.

Following the joint graduation ceremony of my two schools, I returned to school number two where we had another ceremony for the students who would be moving into "junior high" level and the junior high students who would be moving on. This was a touching event held in a small conference room, where teachers gave the equivalent of graduation addresses to the students. Generally, Thais do not display emotion, so I was touched and surprised when one of the male teachers choked up during his speech.

Then all of the students lined up and paraded before the faculty to receive "good luck" wishes with the customary tying of a piece of string around the wrist. Some went away with dozens of strings circling their wrists. All the while, the remaining students were kneeling before us on the floor, awaiting a turn at having a good-luck string patiently tied around a wrist. Kuhn Somlak, school director and my particular benefactor, had tears streaming some of the time as she embraced those students moving on. She is a very special lady.

I should mention that much picture-taking goes on throughout the day. Once the ceremony was completed, teachers and dignitaries posed with the respective groups for a class photograph. I was included among the honored guests in all of this ceremony and was privileged to be among them. People display a great deal of gratitude to have me here and I'm anxious to live up to their expectations. It is a great learning experience for me, not only on the teaching side, but on the cultural and social side. This is a fascinating society to study and to write about.

The Sound of Music (or Is It?)

I chose to live on the outskirts of town in hopes of having relative quiet, but there is no way. Last weekend there was a wedding party at a wat two blocks distant from my house. I appreciate a party as much as the next person—but for two days at full blast!

Loudspeakers came into play by 9 a.m. No intermissions were evident throughout the day. There seems to be a cultural "love me, love my music" consensus. The capacity for hearing ones own voice at full volume is boundless and matched with energy to keep the pace. The most insignificant gatherings require massive loudspeakers and fervent karaoke performances. More than once I have wished myself invisible and in possession of wire cutters.

I did have the foresight to bring to Thailand quality foam earplugs, but absolutely nothing deadens the eternal thump, thump of bass instruments. They literally vibrate the atmosphere, if not the earth. The wedding party in question finally died down about midnight Saturday—only to start up again at 5 a.m. on Sunday morning and continue throughout the day.

On any given Sunday, there is an ordination party on the road located across a plowed field from my house. Often, a twenty-one-year-old male decides to enter priesthood. It could be for three months, three years or forever. For most, it lasts only three months, during the Lenten period. "Ordination helps to bring the youth nearer to the path of virtue, because by ordination they will at least learn, through study, how to do good and avoid evil, and how to curb their passions, especially at the age when these passions are usually strongest."

LORETTA J. DUNBAR

I have seen youths carried overhead to the wat by family and friends along the route, or riding in the back of a pick-up truck. Whichever the case, there is singing and jigging throughout the parade of well-wishers, presumably beginning at the youth's home and heading toward the wat of his choice. My first warning is the discordant sound of keyboard and drums in the distance over the ever-present portable loudspeaker mounted on a two-wheel carriage and rolled along the route. Perhaps there is a 'loud-speaker-for-hire' entrepreneur in the town. It usually takes thirty minutes for the party to pass my area and fade to insignificance.

What prompts today's dissertation is a party in progress about 150 meters from my house. It began early this morning—it is now 5 p.m. At about 1 p.m. the loudspeakers were disengaged. Hey, not guilty. I haven't even bought wire cutters yet. Perhaps the rental on the speakers ran out, or maybe other neighbors are as unhappy as I with the unnecessary sound volume, and registered complaint. Of course, if they were blasting country western music by Alan Jackson or George Strait I'd probably be a tad more tolerant. Yet even that would drive me up a wall after a few hours—and it is never "a few" hours here.

In my three months in Thailand, I've participated in two parades, witnessed several festivals, ordination parades and many other celebratory occasions, and the sound rarely varies. There is no tune, no melody—just an incessant, droning beat. It is not unlike the sounds I experienced on the African continent over thirty years ago, and I suspect exists in many cultures. These cross-cultural discords are rare, but they do exist. It would be unrealistic not to expect them. I've been sound-sensitive since early childhood, and I came into this service knowing it would be one of my several hurdles. I surprise even myself with my patience (hard won over years of maturation). I just hope it doesn't fail me for at least the next two years. It does warp a little now and then.

Oh, blast! The loud speaker has just been reinstated. Another night for earplugs.

Parade of Kings

Uthai Thani has the distinction of being the birthplace of the father of the first king of the Chakri Dynasty—that of the present king. There is a beautiful monastery atop a nearby hill with 449 steps leading from the base to the top of the hill. One can also drive to the top by road. Next to the monastery stands an elegant four-sided Thai-style pavilion housing the monument of Pra Prathom Borom Maha Chanok, the great grandfather of the present Chakri Dynasty which began in 1782.

April 6, 2004, was Memorial Day for the father of King Rama I. I had been alerted a couple weeks earlier that I was invited to participate in a parade that day. My co-teachers know that I haven't any dressy Thai clothes as yet, but they want me in Thai dress. One thing leads to another. First, a teacher offers me a length of Thai silk cloth—enough for a skirt. Then Jirapa suggests that her sister, who works for a dressmaker, could sew the skirt. But what about a blouse? Sister finds some spare cuttings with which to fashion a blouse. The next thing I know, I am being measured for custom-made clothes. One measuring, no fittings, and the finished product arrives at my door minutes before needed for the parade. Everything fits beautifully.

I was duly picked up by the directors of my two schools—a married couple—a few minutes before starting time. It was obvious that I cannot ride my bike wearing a stylish, slim-line silk skirt. In fact, I was often picked up by automobile for various outings throughout the weeks. The beautiful Somluk was wearing a pale peach silk dress and carrying a matching umbrella to ward off the punishing sun. Apparently I passed muster, for my fellow teachers (who also walked in the parade) seemed to approve of my attire, and many photos were taken along the way.

When marching music heralded the start of the parade, I was blown away when I recognized the Marine Hymn. That sure got my attention. I wondered where I was for a minute. Thereafter, there was Thai music only.

Reigning King Bhumibol (Rama IX) is the ninth in the Chakri Dynasty. In the parade, each of the nine kings was represented by a large framed portrait. Each king had his entourage—some coming from regions quite distant from Uthai Thani.

The parade began with dozens of walkers carrying tall poles from which hung beautiful woven banners representative of the various weaving regions of the province. The portraits of the kings began with Rama I. Each segment was accompanied by Thais wearing a variety of garments representing wearing apparel down through the ages. There were also Thai dancers, as well as a group of school children dressed in costume and striking typical Thai poses. It took about an hour and a half for all of the royal portraits to reach the end of the parade route. My school group marched with those representing Rama III, so we reached the foot of the mountain in good time to stand and watch the remainder of the parade to its end. We took shelter under a tree and consumed cold water by the liter. Most of the ladies in the parade carried umbrellas against the sun, me included.

In this tremendous heat, none of my crowd attempted to walk up the 449 steps to the mountain top. However, we later learned that the mayor of the province made it half way up before fainting and being taken to hospital. There is a saying in Great Britain that only "mad dogs and Englishmen go out in the mid-day sun". A very apt saying.

Several kings left their mark in memorable ways, and are well remembered in the history books for their achievements. No matter where you look, you will find the likeness of King Bhumibol, often along with his family, mounted at the highest place in the room—very near the ceiling.

This is just the beginning of what to me could prove to be an almost unbearably hot summer season. It didn't take long for me to begin thinking of where I would escape to next year at this time. Alaska was sounding pretty good. Though a visit to New Zealand holds a great deal of appeal and is closer.

Thai New Year

A deep orange harvest moon hovers above the horizon and day threatens to break within the hour. It is not yet six in the morning and it is easily in the 80s Fahrenheit. I have opened the bedroom window to let in what passes for fresh air. I have a strong signal from BBC World Service on my short-wave radio and the trusty oscillating fan is whirring away.

Folks in Augusta, Georgia, are preparing for world-class golfers to arrive for the Masters Golf Tournament and Easter week is approaching in much of the world. Here in Thailand, everyone is preparing for Songkran Festival.

Songkran is one of the old Thai New Years. They have two old New Years: one was estimated according to the solar system, and the other one to the lunar system. Songkran falls on April 13, 14 and 15 each year. On approximately the 15th the sun commences its April zodiac. The word Songkran, meaning "step in to join", indicates that the sun, having finished its old course, is about to set on a new one. Thai people do three things during Songkran: merit-making, paying visits to their elders to receive their blessing, and then enjoying themselves. Merit-making is when they give food to the priests, give alms to the poor, and set free some animals, usually birds and fish.

This is a time when Thais return home to visit their elders—not unlike our family reunions in the States. They bring small presents, and water each elder's palm with a few drops of *nahm ob thai*—a homemade scent or lotion—as a sign of their love and respect, while the elders offer blessings in return.

As for enjoying themselves, a peculiar but remarkable custom of Songkran festivals is spraying one another with water, which usually smells sweet with flowers and other Thai scents. If you're out of your house during Songkran festival days, you are sure to be drenched sooner or later.

I was enlisted to participate in a parade during the festival, and duly warned to wear something that isn't 'see-through' when wet. My friendly director, Somlak, bought me an inexpensive opaque, throw-away-quality blouse to ensure my modesty during the parade. In the cities, there is much revelry. Here in the country, I expect a gentler dousing.

Tuesday, April 13, 2004: the day has arrived. Jirapa urged me to start the day at the temple with her family, where she would explain to me what was happening during the ceremony. I was picked up by car before 7:30 a.m., duly dressed in my fine Thai silk skirt and a fresh cotton blouse, because Jirapa requested that I dress in Thai style. (I'm beginning to feel like the organ-grinder's monkey.)

I smile to myself when we get to the temple and find that many people are dressed in everyday clothes—just like church at home. I make the tenth person in the party, along with nine of Jiripa's nearest relatives. Each family is carrying a basket laden with rice, flowers, candles and incense offerings. Along one long wall sit several monks and a goodly number of young saffron-clad, shaven-headed boys, spending their summer holiday in study with the monks. Sort of trying it on for size, I think.

Following the hour-long chanting and prayers, we make our way to a corner café where we breakfast on rice, chicken and soup. The parade is to begin at 3 p.m., so I have some time to return home, water my orchids, do a little needlepoint and try to pretend that I am not growing more lethargic with each rising degree in temperature. By eleven I am ready for a nap! By one, I can no longer put off turning on the little room air-conditioner in my bedroom. How I dread getting out on my bike at 2:30 p.m. for a ride into town, where I will "step in to join" the 2km-walk in the mid-day sun. Sheer madness! By this time I look forward to a good drenching with water.

THAI ODYSSEY

I put on my cheap shirt with a pair of khaki shorts and my Tevas sandals—ready for a dousing of water. I'm not far from home when I receive my first water blast. Kids along the roadside are prepared with water hoses or barrels of water and plastic pails. I actually welcome the first cooling sensation. By the time I make the ten-minute ride to Jirapa's house in town, I am thoroughly soaked. Much more than anticipated. Young people ride around in pick-up trucks carrying huge barrels of water and having water fights all through the main road. All of this feels pretty good until they add powder to the water that leaves a chalky residue on everything.

From Jirapa's house, we go by car to the south end of the main road—the meeting place where the parade is to begin. There we meet up with the school directors and several teachers.

A couple of pick-up trucks carrying statues of Buddha lead the parade, followed by the only real "float" that is graced with several young Thai maidens suitably dressed and made up beautifully. There is also a large ceramic pink pig representing the year of the pig, which is about to begin, and a statue of a monkey representing the year just past. That single float is followed by a rag-tag mob of dancers doing the jig to the very discordant sounds blasting through loud speakers and coming from an electric keyboard. There is no tune, rhyme or reason. The musician, if I may misuse the word, appears to simply hit notes up and down the keyboard at random. Accompanying him is a selection of drums and clangers equally discordant. Ugh, I have forgotten my earplugs in my backpack.

The more uninhibited among the crowd swivel their hips and wave their arms and hands overhead. A few are passing bottles of liquor among themselves. It is definitely a bad idea to walk near me, for I am a prime target for dousing. It goes without saying that I am the only 'farang' in attendance. There are, however, a goodly number of genuinely caring and friendly folks who anoint my palms with scented lotion and wish me a "Happy New Year".

Upon reaching the destination at Five Corners square, where there is a permanent display of mock elephant tusks, we find a sheltered seating area to rest throughout the balance of the spectacle. By this time, I am so thoroughly drenched to the skin and beyond, that the heat has no affect. I feel comfortable.

The end of the performance amounts to giving water and good wishes to a lineup of monks and old folks that are seated along the main roadside, with floral arrangements on a low bench placed in front of them. They sit with open palms and receive water and blessings from the hundreds of well-wishers. When I gaze into those world-weary eyes and see their work-worn hands, I think, "There but for the grace of God go I". I had been invited earlier to sit in the receiving line with the respected old folks, but declined with my customary reply, *mai gaa*, "I'm not old"—yet!

A petite, sweet-faced, white-haired lady preceded me in the line of well-wishers. She chatted with my companion and translator, Jirapa. The following day, Jirapa, said the lady asked about me and about my age. When asked to guess, the lady replied, "fifty or so". I had guessed her to be my age, when in fact she is fifty-five.

I was relieved to have Songkran day behind me—until Jirapa reminded me that I can expect to get a dousing of water every day through the eighteenth—another five days.

When I got home at the end of the day, I found that my once-upon-a-time lily-white bra is variegated blue and that my khaki shorts have vertical blue streaks. Even though I had washed the cheap shirt, blue dye ran all over everything.

Indeed, dousing continued every day. On two days, I braved the streets dressed quite respectably in a skirt and blouse and managed to hold up a hand and say "no" at several dousing areas and got through the day completely dry. However, on the third day I wore shorts and T-shirt and was targeted once again. I had to put my backpack in a plastic bag to avoid damage to it and its contents. I'm more than ever convinced of the wisdom of being on holiday in a distant land next April.

An Ordinary Day

It is 5 a.m., pre-dawn in the hamlet of Uthai Thani. I've been awake for nearly an hour. This is not insomnia; I've simply had a full share of sleeping hours, having been in bed by 8:30 last night.

I sit at my desk at an open window with an oscillating floor fan whirling away in hope of coaxing a whisper of breeze into the room. I have shoved the window screen back to let in the early morning air—before the inevitable burning of trash can fill the atmosphere with flying specks of black soot. The gnats take advantage of access into the bedroom, drawn to the lighted screen of my Toshiba Notebook computer. Because I live in a fishbowl of sorts, I haven't turned on the overhead light. I'm working by the light of the computer screen, which highlights my presence in the room. I'm about fifteen feet from the red-dirt lane in front of my shoebox house. In the distance, I see specks of light from traffic along the bypass road. The world never sleeps.

Zap! That is the demise of a gnat whose pestering finally got the better of me.

Already I hear faint noises from my back neighbors as they prepare to take their wares to the 'morning market'. By 6 a.m. the market will be teeming with sellers and buyers. The silhouette of a rider on bicycle is just passing in the lane—probably on the way to the market. Food shopping is done on a daily basis. Many families either don't have refrigeration, don't have adequate income, or simply purchase provisions each day out of habit and custom. There is no doubt that shopping in the market is a social affair. Gossip is exchanged and secrets revealed. They probably already know that I'm sitting here in front of my computer clad only in a light cotton sarong. My every move is a source of amusement and interest. This doesn't bother me—it is part of the cultural exchange; for I am observing their every move, too. How else could I write these essays? Very little cooking is done at home. The market is overflowing with venders 'woking' or grilling all manner of food all day and evening. I would like to have the plastic bag and rubber band concession in Asia. Squid, shrimp and other delectables brewed in a tasty broth are ladled into plastic bags and secured by rubber band, to be taken home or to work. Every imaginable food combination is available for 'takeout' purchase in a plastic bag.

I have only a portable, single gas burner for cooking, and I've only fired it up about three times in over two weeks. I nearly always have my mid-day meal with fellow teachers at an outdoor restaurant. I make that my main meal and have fruit or something equally light for my evening meal.

The sky is lightening now and foot traffic and motorcycles are beginning to pass my window. I can hear the repetitious slapping of water being tossed off into the nearby ditch by a man living a couple doors to my left. From the looks of the lean-to he lives in I can only guess that there isn't a proper *hong nahm* within, for each morning I hear the disposal of bathwater into the ditch opposite his home. While I was sweeping my cement forecourt yesterday, he was sweeping the dirt road in front of his house. Different economic levels, same housekeeping chores.

This is the time of day that the "for real" birds announce their presence. I used to hear them as I cycled to school in Ban Pong during the training weeks. Their call sounds to me very much like someone shouting "for real", "for real", so I labeled them accordingly. I don't know their true name, what they look like or their size.

There is a slight heat-haze that usually lasts for a couple hours—another reason to be up and about early in the day. When the massive orange sun breaks through, the temperature soars. I'm guessing it to be in the 80s Fahrenheit at the moment. Even that feels cool compared to what it will be by noon.

THAI ODYSSEY

There go four Buddhist monks in the lane, walking one in front of the other, heading for the nearest temple, clad in saffron cloth and carrying begging bowls to receive the daily alms that enable their existence. It must be 6 a.m., for the public address system has just kicked in with the daily news, to be followed by a bit of music and further chatter—in Thai language, of course. Thankfully, the nearest speaker is some distance away, and when my door and windows are closed, I don't really notice it; unlike my homestay room where the speaker was right outside my window.

My house looks neat as a pin; pale blue floor tiles gleam, but a wet mop reveals an overlay of black residue. I have puzzled over the structure of the floor since moving in. The bedroom floor, at the front of the house, is elevated about one inch above the floor of the adjacent living/dining area, which is elevated about one inch above the kitchen floor, which is elevated about one inch above the bathroom floor. The entire floor is tiled. After pondering this scheme for some weeks, I've decided that if rainwater seeps through the windows onto the floor at the front of the house, it will run to the bathroom at the back of the house, where there is a floor drain. Is this genius or coincidence? Clean floors take priority, so perhaps it is all by design. I do know that I must be careful when wandering the house in the middle of the night, for I must remember that little inch-high stumbling block at each doorway if I want to avoid stubbing my toes or falling on my face in the dark.

Look!—there is a sapphire kingfisher just landed on the tiptop of a dead bamboo stalk twenty yards away—he is on the lookout for breakfast. And there!—he's found it and is now perched on a bamboo pole even closer. Now he is off again for second helpings. Other birds that I've yet to identify are awakening with the dawn. There is a bevy of tiny birds, very much like our common house sparrow in the States, that claims my house, front and back—and leaves markings accordingly, including on the seat of my one-speed bicycle parked at the front door.

A low ridge of mountains is now visible in the distance and my stomach reminds me that it is time for breakfast. I found Kellogg's muesli in one of the shops and I usually breakfast on that with yogurt and fruit. I have fresh pineapple ready for eating and a lovely golden mango in reserve. All manner of birdlife is now on the wing in search of morning munchies—and so am I.

At 9:30, the school van with driver, and my two co-teachers, will pick me up for a drive to Nakhon Sawan, 45km north of Uthai Thani, for a shopping spree. It is my nearest city and has a couple of wannabe Wal-Mart-like stores: Big C and Makro—each equally barn-like and uninteresting. No exciting food to be found there. I'm on the lookout for the small, enterprising grocer that might supply exotics such as cheese, peanut butter or canned beans in tomato sauce. What I wouldn't give for a can of corned beef. With luck, I might even find corn chips and salsa (dreamer). However, I expect to trek to Bangkok next week for a day-long search for English-language paperback books and *farang* food. It is a three-hour journey by van each way. Jirapa and I will leave here at 6 a.m. and return before dark.

But now, it is time for breakfast.

Mindset

What silly games our minds play. We go abroad in search of knowledge and experience in a new culture, a different country, far from home and familiar sensations—and then we yearn for that which we happily left behind.

I had an earnest yen for a hamburger the other day. I probably don't eat two a year when at home. I fancied a trip to the "city" for a day of self-indulgence on *farang* food. With the expert instruction by Jirapa's college-aged niece, I was guided to the requisite sites in Bangkok.

Jirapa and I took a 6:15 a.m. van to Bangkok for the day. The 15-seater van was full to capacity (for they don't depart with empty seats). The demand is so great, that there is a van leaving every fifteen minutes from pre-dawn to dusk. It is a tight squeeze, but the van is air-conditioned and the road fairly good. It is a three-hour ride from Uthai Thani to Bangkok. Much time is wasted with bumper-to-bumper traffic at the Bangkok end of the journey.

We finally arrive at Victory Monument that stands in the middle of the spacious square at Snam Pao. The monument was built at the close of the Thai-Viet Nam war on the question of the frontier between the two countries. The base is a decagonal block that is now hollow, but at one time it contained the remains of the national heroes who died in defense of their motherland. You can't help being impressed by its majesty and grandeur, inspired by its lofty bayonet spire and its five man-sized bronze statues depicting army, navy, air force, a policemen and a civilian, each in different postures.

The huge roundabout at Victory Monument is the hub of Bangkok's public transportation system. The van station is located near an entrance to the very efficient elevated Sky Train. Buses heading out in every direction have their assigned stations all around the square. There is an elevated walkway encircling the entire area, with heavy foot traffic of people walking around and then down stairways to their desired bus stop.

We hopped the Sky Train for a ride to the Emporium shopping center, where I found enough food to satisfy my American tastes. My cupboard now boasts Skippy peanut butter, Hormel canned corned beef from Brazil, local brands of baked beans, corn and tuna. And I have cheese and taco shells, but nothing to put in them. There is a Mexican food manufacturer in Bangkok; I just need to find out which shops stock their products. There are many other shopping centers to investigate during future food quests.

I found healthy looking ground beef for sale, but I wasn't properly prepared to carry perishable foods back to Uthai Thani. I will be prepared next time. For the time being, I'll let corned beef substitute for ground beef and dip into my one and only packet of Taco mix (brought with me from Aiken), and I'll soon have tacos prepared with local tomatoes and lettuce. With the remaining corned beef, I'll prepare a meal of corned beef hash, using my one remaining potato and an onion, topped with a fried egg. I'll easily get two meals from one can of corned beef.

Adjacent to the grocery section are the ever-present KFC, Burger King and Dairy Queen, along with Thai-food restaurants and a tempting bakery. I headed straight for Burger King. One cheeseburger and a Sprite later, I was completely satisfied to do without for another couple of months, maybe years. The yen had been satisfied, and my mindset was at ease.

Before we went food shopping, I was guided to a second-hand book store just down the road from the Emporium—that was our primary destination, even before food. I sighed with relief to find stacks of paperback novels in English—looking very much like any second-hand book shop at home. I won't invest in a television set here, and the shortwave radio broadcasts are spotty and often filled with static, so my chief relaxation is reading. Now I know where I can get my fix.

So there we are, I can purchase all of my comfort requirements within three hours of home. I probably won't go into Bangkok more than once a quarter to stock up, but it is a comfort just to know I can do it in a day—anytime. In between times, I'll enjoy tasty Thai and Chinese cuisine from the market food stalls and I'll savor the tropical fruits that abound.

Postscript: I just finished a lunch of corned beef hash. I miss the heavy iron skillet I use at home, but the tinny fry pan I have here did the job. I forgot to look for mustard yesterday, but will put that on my next list.

This little venture has brought me around to the teachings of Buddha, who believed that the main cause of all suffering springs from nothing but our ever-increasing desire; the desire to possess what seem to us pleasurable, and to avoid what seem to be unpleasant. He finally found that the best way to success was "The Middle Way"— that is, avoiding the two extremes of indulging oneself in pleasures or torturing oneself to the utmost.

While I live a relatively Spartan existence here, I feel that I'm already gathering too many material possessions, and am over-indulging in foodstuffs. The simple life has such great appeal. Just now my oscillating fan developed a whirring noise—too great to tolerate. It must go for repairs. Oh, the bother of material possessions. Without it, I'm in a heavy sweat, but how do I transport it to the repairman by bicycle. Where is the middle way when I need it?

To the rescue: Jirapa arrived for a visit; I explained my plight, and we cycled to the nearest electric shop, where I purchased a new fan. The fan was delivered to my house immediately, and the older fan was taken back for repair. My "middle way" was provided by one of my many kind Thai friends, who always seem to be able to solve these minor annoyances with grace. Everyone knows everyone and they all look out for one another.

Postscript II: I did have my tacos with corned beef and they were delicious. I did, however, miss the requisite taco sauce. Never mind, they were still a treat. A day later I had a bacon, lettuce and tomato sandwich—spectacular.

Indulgence at Iyara Park

In May 2001 I took myself on a tour of French villages to celebrate my 70th birthday. The following year I did a walking tour in the Czech Republic, and celebrated my 71st birthday with new travel companions. Last year I made a belated trip to Costa Rica. Let's just say that I've made it a habit to spend my birthday abroad. I don't like birthdays. Who does! Except that we celebrate making it out of bed yet another 365 days in a row.

This May I'm already abroad, so I thought to go from the ridiculous (present living conditions) to the sublime (Iyara Park). Iyara Park is only 10km from my tiny house in Uthai Thani. The venue is magnificence personified. The structure is built in a square design that allows an atrium to exist within, as well as a swim area that would be insulting to call a 'pool'. It took ten years—parcel by parcel—to accumulate the total of 250 acres, and to build the hotel resort. Throughout that time the grounds staff fashioned a magnificent and fanciful topiary garden that I delighted in photographing in the early morning light. It took about seven years to complete the resort.

There is a statuary family of twenty-one life-size cement elephants cavorting at a watering hole, and other elephant images scattered around the grounds in various poses, my favorite being a mother and baby elephant bursting up through a mock segment of stone paving blocks.

The hotel resort is palatial in every aspect. The décor is minimal in the way of oriental taste. A handsome pair of life-size elephant statues guards the vestibule, and others are found on the ground level floor along with tasteful Thai-culture specimens. I don't want to sound like a PR rep, so I'll just mention that there are about 400 rooms, and the grounds include an 18-hole golf course, tennis courts, and all the amenities you might expect to find, with a price tag of ten million dollars in building costs.

I stayed only twenty-four hours, but made the most of it. Best of all, it was a treat to be in full air-conditioning for a day and have dry skin all the while; nary a drop of perspiration. I had a Thai massage that lasted for an hour and a quarter for $2.55. The following morning I had a manicure, pedicure, shampoo and haircut for $15. The overnight stay cost the equivalent of a month's Peace Corps salary—and it was worth every baht. Needless to say, I went the plastic route for this little splurge.

The really pitiful aspect is that this property sits in the middle of nowhere on the road to nowhere. It is beautifully and solidly constructed and tasteful in every way. Location, location, location, as any real estate agent will murmur. I don't know details, but I am told that the Thai owner is a woman in the export trade. There are hundreds of staff for the gardens alone. The up-side is that Iyara supports a multitude of needy Thais, and that alone makes it viable in my book. I couldn't get a booking until they were expecting a tour group and were staffed up accordingly.

The property remains closed for all practical purposes between large bookings. The day I dropped in for a 'look-see' a month earlier, there was a good sampling of staff in place, but not a single guest.

Would I do it again? Maybe. The English-speaking tourist hasn't discovered Iyara Park yet in May 2004. There were fifty rooms occupied by Thais from Bangkok having a long May Day weekend outing when I was there. I was the only 'European'. I'm getting used to being the only non-local wherever I go. The Thai people are so darn charming. The best English speakers were assigned to attend me. One girl was a Filipino married to a Thai and was thrilled to show me the works and to practice English language with me. My gentleman wait-staff in the dining room was as thin as a reed, with a glorious smile. His

English was superior, and mostly self-taught via BBC radio and cassette tapes.

I enjoyed the pampering: the meals where I could sit down to a table setting that included a table knife among the cutlery, the clean, cool air, spotless housekeeping, two hot showers and an hour-long hot tub of bubbles—during which I worked the Bangkok Post crosswords while soaking. But it is living in a vacuum.

Remember the stale joke about 'how many blankety-blank does it take to replace a light bulb?' Well, how many Thais does it take to get Loretta to the resort? You can't get through the gate without a reservation. All of my Thai friends wanted entry. We were six in the car that took me, and seven on the return trip—thank goodness for the short distance. Lots of picture taking ensued. Admittedly, I had a momentary mindset shift upon departing Iyara for my return to the shoebox.

Late in the afternoon of my return, we had a weather change that began with a big blow that had plastic debris swirling and red dust sieving through the window screens, followed by the first big rain since I moved to Uthai Thani. I quickly learned that my house is not waterproof—some leakage around the windows. Thank goodness the house slants toward a floor drain in the rear. Back to real life at its basic level.

I'm not sure what the moral to this story is, but I see it this way: I'm only ten minutes away from the 'good life'. That makes it a lot easier to tolerate and to enjoy life on a dusty lane in a little out-of-the-way-town filled with thoughtful, generous and caring people. The contrast is remarkable and I'm privileged to have access to the best of both worlds.

Home Improvements

Things have improved a little at my house. When I lamented the fact that I had such an uncomfortable west facing that I couldn't even have orchid plants because they would shrivel in the heat, the school directors immediately arranged to have a shelter built on my cement forecourt by the school maintenance men. I had in mind having a small thatched canopy made of bamboo under which I could hang orchid plants and which would also shade the living room window from the deadly afternoon sun. Two days later, however, there appeared at my door an acetylene torch and great lengths of metal tubing. The shelter would cost nothing using these spare materials from the school.

Not the aesthetic affect I had in mind, but 'gift horse, etc.' The shelter is about eight-feet square and has blue netting over the top. Not a thing of beauty, but it does protect plants and reduce the setting sun coming into the living room. Hopefully, when the dreadful summer is over, it may be pleasant to sit out there now and then. Unfortunately, the metal handle at the glass front door into the house is still too hot to touch in the late afternoon without an oven glove.

One day I realized that an opaque curtain at the back kitchen window would give me a little privacy to prowl the kitchen scantily clad in the evenings, so I found the fabric and the wire and eye screws to make this improvement. I can still keep the louvers open for air circulation. Unfortunately, I didn't have a hammer to ease the screws into hardwood window frames. However, I was very determined, and with the aid of the awl feature of my Swiss Army knife, I finally forced the issue. The curtain not only gives me privacy when back-lit at night, but it also cuts down the dust and soot that filters through the open louvers. It is only a half-curtain (lower half), but is just what I need. I took the fabric to a local dressmaker and had her seam it up to my prescribed dimensions.

During a recent shopping trip to Nakhon Sawan (35km) in the school van, I found a tiny toaster oven. It has no thermostat, just an on/off dial with a 15-minute timer. Baking a potato is tricky; I cut it in half lengthwise so it will cook more quickly. It makes passable toast and I can re-heat leftovers.

On the way home from the post office last week, there was a roadside vender selling the exact bookcase I had been looking for. I have a couple like it in Aiken. It is a sturdy wooden three-shelf, folding book case. I stopped to inquire the price. When I motioned that I was *kee jak a yan*, 'riding a bike', and obviously unable to transport the bookcase, the vender volunteered to put my bike and the bookcase in his pick-up truck and take us home. I was delighted with this unexpected addition to my meager furnishings. It is little surprises like this that keep me going.

My good friend, Jirapa, has several relatives who live in Bangkok. When I admired her mother-in-law's floor lamp (mother-in-law is a neighbor of mine) I was told that her niece could bring me a lamp from Bangkok. Sure enough, a week later the niece arrived at my doorstep with a lovely floor lamp for my bedroom. What a delight not to have to use ceiling lights to read by in bed at night. When I'm feeling flush one day, I'll have her bring another one for the lounge area. Right now there is no furniture there anyway. That same niece went away today with a 'wish list' of *farang* food to be hunted down in Bangkok for me. She looked quite dismayed at the list—what in the world is corned beef, salsa? I described at length what some of these bizarre foods are like, but told her *mai pen rai*, 'never mind', if you can't find them.

My latest home improvement is the installation of a hot water heater. I expect you're envisioning a well insulated 40-gallon tank. This, however, is the European variety that you might have encountered in small guest houses. It is smaller than a shoe box and

THAI ODYSSEY

is mounted adjacent to the shower head. It is simply a powerful emersion heater. The cold water is heated before it reaches the showerhead. It takes no time at all and is totally effective. You realize, of course, that there is only one water pipe—cold water. The tap is labeled 'H2O'. Thus, there is no hot water at the basin or at the kitchen sink.

My latest refinement is that Jirapa arranged for the local news seller to deliver the Bangkok Post to my door early each day. Now that is service. It happens that the delivery boy passes my house when making a delivery to a school down the road. It saves me an out-of-the-way bike ride.

Oh, drat! It is Friday afternoon and I'm hearing the dreaded bass rhythm from the wat down the road. Please don't tell me they are warming up for another weekend of 'the sound of music'.

Postcript: I received my wish-list of food from Bangkok a week later. My friend did a great job. Some of the items are not exactly what I expected, but *mai pen rai*. I have a large jar of pickled vegetables and a two-year supply of French's mustard; the rest worked out pretty well. I ate tacos last night with real hamburger. I have salsa and chips on tap for another time.

Entertainment Center

There is a squeak, squawk and hum from my trusty, thirty-year-old Grundig portable radio with its shortwave, mid-wave and FM broadcast bands. Forget the mid-wave and FM bands—never anything found on them. But thank goodness for shortwave. My strongest reception comes from BBC World News; a close second is Canadian broadcasting, with Voice of America a weak third. BBC has good variety as well as long broadcast hours. Canada is very interesting, as it comes from a North American point of view that isn't that of the United States. Voice of America is a bit of a disappointment.

What a treat and surprise to catch a few minutes of Kenny Chesney's country/western sound at 5:30 a.m. one day. I was never again able to find that station. Sometimes Australia and New Zealand have strong signals. Unfortunately, there are no English-language music broadcasts on any band. China has a strong English broadcast from time to time and is fairly interesting. And so, the Grundig is my chief 'entertainment center'. Many days, signal interference is intrusive, but I tweak until I find something worth listening to.

Under the heading of 'entertainment' I must include the Bangkok Post newspaper. I sometimes spend a good part of the afternoon reading articles and doing the crossword puzzle. So far, I have successfully completed the words once and I've come within just two words of completion a couple of times. It is just enough to goad me on each day. The puzzle authors are British, but that is okay. After twenty-seven years with Hamish, my Scots husband, I feel pretty comfortable with British thinking.

Each week, Peace Corps sends out Newsweek magazine to every volunteer worldwide. I received it in the African bush thirty-three years ago in Ghana. It must be remembered that there are different versions going out to the various continents of the world—not always the same as found in the United States.

I probably miss country/western music most of all. I transferred some music from CDs at home onto my laptop computer which, by the way, is my only speaker system—but not bad for a small computer. And then my dear friend and neighbor in Aiken sent me seven country/western disks—nice birthday gift. I haven't invested in a boom box, because there is not enough English language available to make it worthwhile. In my tiny house it would be too much sound anyway.

I must include my laptop as a part of my entertainment center, for I am guilty of playing solitaire or Mah Jongg for a short while in the late evenings, before bedtime. Most of all, it is wonderful to have it for writing these essays. I bought my first CVD on a visit to Bangkok last month. The only thing I found in English that I hadn't already seen was a sci-fi piece with Sean Connery. His name alone sold me; can't resist that Scottish accent. It is not easy to come across English language CVDs, but I recently discovered the local rental store. Most titles are not what I'd choose normally, and there are a very few that aren't dubbed in Thai, so I take what I can get.

Probably my most reliable form of entertainment is reading an eclectic selection of paperback books. I grow panicky when I have fewer than six books in reserve on the bookshelf. That is about the time I plan a visit to Bangkok and The Elite Used Books shop near the Emporium shopping center.

I most certainly don't miss American television. Thai TV is even worse.

My constant entertainment is the world around me: the culture, the people, the everyday act of planning a meal for the day, walking through the market and being 'eyed' and 'eying' right back, always on the watch for something I might have missed before. I saw a lovely little head of cauliflower this morning and was about to pick it up when I spotted a healthy green worm working its way out of a crevice. It put me off cauliflower for the day.

Last, but not least is a small needlepoint piece I brought with me from Aiken. I'm pacing myself so that it should last two years. During the workweek I have little spare time for such luxuries, but come the weekends I enjoy all of the above.

Time to tune into BBC and get the news headlines on the half hour.

Kitchen Foray

I have explained before that many European and American food products and other items are available in Bangkok. But Bangkok can seem a million miles away. In fact, for many volunteers it is too far to journey except on orders from Peace Corps on rare occasions. Therefore, one of our challenges is to improvise.

I was hungry for pickles. We have beautiful baby cucumbers here. I certainly don't have the means for pickling, but I recalled my mother preparing thinly sliced pickled cucumbers, so I dug into my memory bank. First, I sliced the cucumbers very thinly and placed them in a bowl of salted water. This apparently neutralizes any bitterness. I let them soak in this brine awhile, then rinsed and drained the slices and patted them dry before adding some vinegar and sugar, and then let it sit while I prepared my lunch.

For lunch I had one remaining baking potato (grown in Chiang Mai) and two tiny chicken tenders left from a visit to Nahkon Sawan two weeks earlier. Wouldn't a tossed salad go nicely with that combination? I've mentioned that I have a mini toaster/oven that has no thermostat—only a fifteen minute timer. First I cut in two, lengthwise, my beautiful potato, and oiled the two halves liberally with Filippo Berio Virgin Olive Oil (my grateful find in the department store this morning), placed them face down on the metal cooking tray, put the tray in the oven and set the timer. While the potato was baking, I prepared a salad dressing of olive oil, vinegar (had to settle for 5% white; no wine vinegar available), minced garlic, a drop of honey and a sprinkling of lemon/pepper seasoning (brought from home) and a squeeze of lime.

By golly, it was right tasty. It made a good marinade for the chicken, too, which went into the oven along side the potato halves for another fifteen minutes. Sadly, my lettuce was no longer useable, so marinated tomatoes were substituted. Ummh, also very tasty. I washed it down with iced green tea with honey and then indulged in chocolate crème Oreo cookies for dessert.

It wasn't gourmet eating, but it surpassed the offer of sticky rice and mango salad by my friend, though that too is a favorite. I have a few slices of bacon and some cheese left from *farang* shopping, and then it is back to Thai basics until the next distance-shopping trip.

Time to check the pickled cucumber slices. Well, I had to dilute the vinegar and sugar solution with a little water, but otherwise they taste almost like mother used to make.

Did I mention that I made tacos with corned beef last week? I missed the taco sauce, but they were a wonderful success, and I have supplies for a couple more meals. So, all is not bleak here. When I can't face another bowl of rice, I resort to a peanut butter and jam sandwich.

I discovered a reasonable facsimile of flour tortillas in the market on Sunday. This variety is wafer thin, like a crepe. There must be endless uses for these as wraps. The other night, I spread one with peanut butter, sprinkled with cinnamon and sugar, rolled it like a cigar and it was fine. They definitely warrant experimentation.

If you grow totally bored, and wonder why in the world I'm going on about food preparation, I'll tell you. The longer my mind is engrossed in the act of writing, the longer I can tolerate sitting bathed in sweat and avoid turning on the air-conditioner. I haven't had my first electric bill yet, and I expect it may be a doozie. I reserve A/C luxury for the late afternoon, evening and for sleeping. I do know that one of these days I won't need it at all, and I live for the day.

At last, classes have resumed and I can finally get down to work. I am conferring with co-teachers, working on lesson plans and reading through the wealth of material provided by Peace Corps. Writing these essays is pure luxury, and soon enough there will be little of note to write about, nor time to do it—so I'm stretching it.

THAI ODYSSEY

I think I'll turn on the A/C and read a bit of Geoffrey Archer's "The Burma Legacy". Seems an appropriate title, since I'm right next door to Burma. I found the book in Bangkok a couple of weeks ago and it is just about time to return for another load of paperbacks.

Postscript: My first electric bill was 733 baht ($18.50); hefty, but manageable, and worth every baht. My Bangkok friends that visit Uthai Thani twice a month have re-provisioned me a second time and I've had tacos with proper ground beef, and salsa with corn chips. Not TexMex quality, but good substitutes. Add a bottle of Thai beer to wash it down, and all is well.

Thai Silk

Weavers from nearby villages travel to Uthai Thani once a month to display and sell their cloth. Thai silk is world renown, but few people have seen how it is made. As a trained and qualified weaver in the French-tapestry-style of weaving myself, I was excited to pay a visit to local weavers. After visiting a workshop, I will never again quibble over the cost of a length of silk cloth woven in Thailand.

It was a hot, dry, dusty day in April—mid-summer in Thailand. We drove about twenty miles into the countryside, passing many fallow rice fields that awaited the rainy season to produce their next crop. My friend and guide knew the way. Soon, we arrived at a nondescript building about the size of a small high school gym. We sought shelter for the car. The owner of the mill greeted us and allowed us free reign, willingly answering our questions. Working conditions were barebones basic. I doubt they had changed in generations, eons. Concrete walls rose half way to the ceiling and from there continued upward with wire mesh. Fans whirled overhead. The roof was corrugated iron and no insulated drop ceiling. It was near 100°F outside, and not a lot cooler inside.

In a tiny showroom area hung lengths of cloth in the vibrant colors favored by Thais, as well as more neutral shades. The most costly of the fabrics are those with ornate hem trims, ranging up to twenty inches in depth. I had presumed that the solid cloth of a garment was machine made and only the attached, decorative lower portion was hand-woven on these looms. Not so. Every centimeter is hand loomed. This accounts for the varying widths of the cloth; sometimes a yard, sometimes a meter or somewhere in between. This is not a mechanized, 'cut-and-dried' operation. These are works of art—wearable art. This is a cottage industry throughout the country.

I was anxious to have a look at the looms—dozens of them were set up in the large, airless building. The weavers were having a holiday for Songkran Festival week, but one lonely weaver was at her loom. We were indeed in luck. The looms looked jerry-built to the untrained eye—so very basic. But the complicated warp threading was precise; the sheds were firm and the shed sticks worn smooth by years of use. The weaver was working on an intricate, decorative pattern about a yard wide. Every strand of weft was being hand-thrown through the shed. She was able to produce about one centimeter along the width of the fabric in a working day. Oh, so painstaking.

I was relating to her every move. My own Aubusson-type tapestry wall hangings are far too labor-intensive to be sold. Only my family are gifted with small samplings; the majority hang in my Aiken home. For me, weaving is a labor of love, a cherished pastime. For this woman, it is her livelihood. I thought of weavers down through the ages who worked under these very same conditions—some coping with cold rather than heat—in rough workshops or cottages throughout the French countryside. The craft, or art, hasn't changed in all these centuries, nor have working conditions improved.

From this workshop, we were taken to another shed where only cotton cloth is produced. Much of this cloth is used for domestic items. However, they do a limited amount of the intricate and decorative cloth used for clothing. This, too, appeals to me, for I find cotton more comfortable to wear.

I came away with great admiration for Thai weavers and their beautifully woven fabrics. I will take my time in selecting colors that suit me and hope to have garments made of both cotton and silk to take home in a couple of years. With any luck, I'll have an opportunity to visit weaving workshops in other regions of Thailand, where patterns and styles vary.

Another rewarding outing on a hot April afternoon.

Thai Massage

Before moving to Thailand, I was led to believe that there was a masseuse in every hamlet. So I inquired where I might get a massage in Uthai Thani. I was told that massage is available only at hospitals for therapeutic needs. After further inquiry, a friend of a friend suggested a visit to the small town of Thap Than about 25km away. It was worth a try—and another source of material for an essay.

Jirapa and I decided to head out into the countryside this week. First, I rode my bike to her house in town; then the two of us biked to the bus station to find the correct *songtao* to Thap Than. A *songtao* might be described as a long-bed pick-up truck with padded bench seats on either side. They serve the outlying villages. The trick is to get on the right one. We found our vehicle and headed out. It was only 9:30 a.m., but the temperature was edging into the 90s. Air passing through the carriage was like a blast furnace.

One fellow passenger is taking home two large, wooden window shutters. They lay in the aisle between the benches. We have no choice but to put our feet on them. About half way to our destination we stop to pick up a farmer who then proceeds to load on six large, bags of 'top seed'. Ours is the next stop and we have no idea what to expect.

What a joyful surprise. Here in this town less than half the size of Uthai Thani, maybe about eight thousand inhabitants, is a pristine medical center. It has a large campus with housing for the doctors, nurses and other essential medical staff. I eye the housing with envy and would love to have one of the small two-story bungalows in Uthai Thani. Everything is freshly painted and the grounds manicured and well kept.

We walk into the reception of the hospital and I am taken aback by the modern air-conditioned facility; very clinical, yet inviting; conveying a feeling of confidence in the services offered. We are directed to another building several meters distant. It is obstructed from view by a hedgerow, so we are again surprised to find a nine-month-old modern building dedicated to only therapeutic massage. We are met by charming young staff who are expecting us. Our details were taken for permanent files. We choose the full body massage with an added herbal treatment.

Attendants hand us cotton, pajama-like garments to change into, and we are ushered into a comfortable air-conditioned treatment room with windows on three sides. All rooms are glass-walled and visible by all and sundry. And then the work begins. This is a very slow, deep massage method meant to relax the muscles. We are treated from toes to head. The treatment takes two full hours and is actually relaxing. We pay the fee of 300 baht ($7.60) and consider it money well spent.

It was by that time twelve-thirty and the sun was at its zenith killing temperature. We faced the thirty-minute *songtao* ride back to Uthai Thani, where we grabbed a quick plate of fried rice from the food stand where we had parked our bikes under the protective eye of the shop owners—parents of former students. Refreshed with a liter of ice water, we again mounted our respective bikes and headed home.

We subsequently located a traditional massage parlor in Uthai Thani town and made good use of it at a later date.

Saturday Night in Uthai Thani

It is 7:45 a.m. on a Sunday. My three adjacent neighbors and a couple more beyond, each have their TV or radio tuned to a different station, and the daily public address system is going strong. I'm tuned to BBC World Service. I've been up for two hours. It is close to impossible to sleep after 5:30 a.m., when my neighbors are sweeping, calling to one another and generally starting their day. I've showered, dressed, eaten, swept the house and forecourt, watered orchids and organized my deskwork for the day. It is muggy as heck and my clothes feel damp and clingy.

But this essay is about last night. It seems that we have finally broken the back of summer and entered an early phase of the rainy season. Often as not, the sky becomes overcast in early afternoon and rain clouds begin to build. Occasionally they pass by without shedding a drop. But you can't be sure. I bring the bicycle into my empty living room to keep it dry. I have a permanent stash of past issues of the Bangkok Post on the floor just under the living room window, and another pile similarly placed at the kitchen window. After a rain, I remove the wet sheets and toss them out. There is no way to plug the window leaks, and this seems the safest way to keep from having water damage. My landlady thinks this is a very clever solution. Now that the season is upon us, I must always close all windows before leaving the house.

I had a hankering for a banana split as a substitute for supper yesterday, because I'd had a healthy salad lunch consisting of lettuce, tomato, tuna chunks, pickle, cucumber, Ranch Dressing and wedges of toasted whole grain bread; I finished off with papaya and a squeeze of fresh lime and washed it down with iced green tea.

LORETTA J. DUNBAR

By the way, when I bring fresh produce home from the market, the first thing I do is fill a basin with water and a teaspoon of Clorox and soak, wash and rinse everything. I place the loose lettuce leaves in a 'basket' made from a couple of sheets of the Bangkok Post Classified Section and give it a good shake to extract the excess water from the leaves before refrigeration.

At 4:30 p.m. I eyed the threatening clouds and calculated my chances of getting to the ice cream shop in town on my bike and back home again before a deluge hit. Okay, let's try. As I neared the shop ten minutes down the road, the clouds grew darker, but I was salivating for ice cream.

Blast it! The ice cream shop was closed; of all the nerve. Plan B: stop at Seven-Eleven and pick up something. I grabbed a couple of individual ice cream cups from the freezer. Ice cream and some of the popcorn I purchased a couple of weeks earlier would make a fine Saturday night supper. Then I raced ahead of the clouds and reached home minutes before a great downpour. I was thankful that the ice cream shop had been closed.

I had a couple of CVD disks in reserve for the weekend. There are hundreds of titles available at the local shop, but only a small percentage has original English sound tracks. Most are dubbed in Thai language. Thus, the selection is limited in the extreme. I have viewed plots I wouldn't touch at home.

I had my doubts about the local brand of popcorn, but "nothing ventured..." Pour a little oil in the saucepan, light the gas burner, add the corn kernels and hope for the best. To my surprise and delight, I've never had a better batch of popcorn from the best brands in America; barely a half dozen un-popped kernels.

Now to settle in for an evening's entertainment. Since my only soft seating is still at the foot of my bed with my back leaning on a plump bed pillow propped against the wall, I set the scene. Place the Toshiba notebook computer on the bed beside me and bring in a tray with a bowl of popcorn and a glass of water; don't forget the ice cream. Darn! I had picked up frozen Slurpys instead of ice cream. Oh, well.

THAI ODYSSEY

I settled in for an hour and a half of "City by the Sea" with Robert DeNiro and some unknowns. The popcorn was great and a coffee-flavored Slurpy was passable. The CVD was better than nothing on a rainy Saturday night in the country. It is a real step up from Saturday nights spent deep in the rainforest of Ghana over thirty years ago. The electronic age has changed all that and it is not realistic to make comparisons. I loved my service in West Africa. It is like making lemonade from lemons. We do what we can with what we have and make the best of it. Every day is a challenge, and that is why I'm here; that's my motivation.

It is 9:00 a.m. and time to take a bike ride into town for the Sunday edition of the Bangkok Post and the two crosswords that will be my afternoon's entertainment.

People on My Street

I live just off the central artery of the town, running north to south. I live at the far north end; the post office is in the distant south. I bike down this long stretch of road and observe the folks living on either side each day. Once I became familiar with the direct route, I began exploring the many narrow back lanes for a change. This is what I see:

A block down from my house, there is a modest garden patch; rich black soil and striking green vegetation. A couple of women in long sleeves, long skirts and straw hats squat and plant or harvest. A young man wearing a wooly stocking cap (no matter the temperature) waters by hand. We nod hello and smile every day of the week. No doubt, this healthy produce reaches the nearby market. A short distance further there is the familiar bamboo platform, about the size of a king-sized bed, in front of a narrow dwelling. There are usually two or three folks lazing there any hour of the day; I nod.

Now I'm on the main road. Students are rushing to school on bicycles; motorcycles are whizzing by, using either side of the road that suits them. I carefully enter the traffic flow on my bike. I feel like one of those bobbing-head dolls you see in diners; I nod my way along the entire route. In one area there is a man living in what is surely a derelict building that must (or should) have been condemned decades ago. Each day, I glance in his open doorway. He is often sitting in his one molded plastic chair in an under vest and shorts; sometimes eating, sometimes sleeping. I can see piles of refuse tossed into the pit nearby where there once must have been flooring. He simply exists from meal to meal, from what I see.

Across the street sits another old gent in a rocker on his front stoop. He is surrounded by, to my mind, junk, but at least he seems to move about some. When he is missing from the stoop, I worry; but then he reappears.

I'm now passing a school. The officer directing traffic nods and calls out, "Kuhn Etta". I met him in the local ice cream parlor one day. I should say here that only in Uthai Thani am I known as Etta. It is very difficult for Thais to say the letters "l" and "r" and they are often used interchangeably. To make it easy on everyone, I lopped off the first three letters of my name and adopted the nickname Etta. Otherwise it was coming out Roletta and variations thereof.

I just passed the old lady who shuffles by my door each day with a bamboo pole across her stooped shoulders and baskets laden with fresh greens hanging at each end. And there goes the rag picker who hovers over the garbage cans at the corner of my street. I save papers and plastic bottles for him. A motorcycle passes me laden with a family of four; a tiny tot sits on a jump seat in front of the driver.

Just outside the news stand, a gentleman nods a greeting; he is a postal clerk who sells me stamps. There is no getting around it; all these friendly nods and greetings add up to a widespread security system for this one lone *farang* lady. The more people that know me, and what I'm doing here, the safer I am. In my very first visit to Uthai Thani, I was introduced at a town meeting, and a councilman admonished the community to look after me.

One day I decided I needed to replace my floor mop, and to buy a large plastic container to store water against the next power failure. I reasoned that I would buy the items, hire a motorized tuk-tuk to carry them home with me, and then bring me back to my bike in town, which I would then pedal home. I made my purchases at the shop where I had purchased many household items in the past, and mimed to the clerk that I would make a brief visit to the market for fresh produce and then return to pick up my purchases and hire a tuk-tuk to take me home.

When I returned from the market, two helpers from the tiny shop were waiting for me with their motorcycle and carrying my mop and large plastic bucket. They motioned me to show them the way to my house. I pedaled as fast as I could down the asphalt in town and over the lumpy dirt lane to my house, and they cycled patiently and slowly behind me and delivered my goods.

These encounters are so very heart-warming and typical of Thai hospitality. I may not know all the people on my street, but most of them seem to know me.

Eating in Interesting Places

During the early days of getting acquainted with my new life in Uthai Thani I observed everything with great interest. The teachers at Wat Kaew are mostly in their forties and are a very compatible lot. During the last two weeks of last school year, when I first arrived, we often went to lunch together in a large group—usually about ten of us. A couple of teachers have vehicles, most others use motorcycles. On one occasion the entire teaching staff of 21 drove 35km into the countryside for an end-of-year celebratory lunch together. When it came time to pay the bill, the three highest paid teachers paid, since they could afford it the most

The first time I tried to contribute my portion of a lunch bill (in true American fashion), it was flatly refused and one of the teachers paid the whole bill. After this happened several times, I asked Jirapa about it. It appears that rather than dithering around with trying to decide who owes what, people take it in turn to pay the bill. They seem to have some method of equalizing the costs that I have yet to discover. I was teased and told that the first time the bill amounts to 2000 baht, I can pay. Gradually, I have managed to host small, spontaneous lunches for three or four at a time. Many of these teachers have been working together for most of their careers and are very good friends. I later learned that it is customary for the highest salaried person in a party to pay the bill. This applies all the time. It pretty well eliminates me from ever paying!

It is the Asian way to order a multitude of dishes to varying tastes, and to share—and what a wild variety appears sometimes. I very much enjoy this version of smorgasbord. There is always something

I can enjoy—and always dishes I'm glad I can decline. I'm sometimes puzzled at the choice of eatery, for very often we end up at an open-air roadside stand with heavy passing traffic, rusted and mismatched chairs and scuffed and wobbly tables. But these strange places are usually known for some particular food or other—not for atmosphere! Thais have healthy appetites. I'm a light eater, and just when I've satisfied my appetite another dish arrives at the table. I know we're coming to the end of a meal when a huge fish is served over a brazier—I'm getting the hang of things. I've eaten more seaweed and undetermined greens than I knew existed, including flower blossoms. I try to be culturally polite, but some dishes just don't work for me.

At one school, there is a monthly luncheon to celebrate all the birthdays for the month. In May, it was a dinner party that combined with a birthday party for me. The directors presented me with the largest orchid plant I have ever seen. It is a hanging plant that measures about forty inches—a third of which is long healthy roots—and deep purple blossoms in a massive bunch at the top.

We gathered at a floating restaurant on the river that flows through the town. Sound exotic? We traversed higgledy-piggledy planks that sank about an inch into the water's edge, in order to reach the restaurant. The furnishings were of the usual mismatched bent and bruised variety, and there were non-matching cloths down the length of the great long table setting for twenty-six. During the course of the meal I glanced up at the bare bulb in the ceiling directly overhead and counted ten geckos enjoying an evening meal of flying insects. At the end of the meal, I and three others were presented with individually personalized birthday cakes.

Houseboats bobbed along the river bank; very rustic, of course. Kids were bathing in the river water and no doubt raw sewage made its way, too. There is no refinement in this setting, but there is an abundance of good cheer, generosity and fun. I was given far more gifts than I can ever account for. More often than not, clothing gifts are too small or too large and likely not to my taste. What to do? I wear them if I can. As I've mentioned in another essay, it doesn't pay to be finicky.

I dare not ponder the condition of restaurant kitchens—a real misnomer. I just know that I see staff squatting at plastic tubs out back and washing the dishes in cold water. I try not to think about the sanitation conditions. If I did, I'd never eat another meal in Thailand. I haven't lost an ounce of weight, despite pedaling each day, and thankfully I haven't gained any either.

School Days

I haven't written about my day in the classroom. Some of the kids are precious—as they are anywhere in the world. There are rudimentary desks and chairs in most of the open-air classrooms and overhead fans whirl at top speed, so that papers, clothing, hair, and anything else loose, goes flying. A real nuisance for everyone, to say the least. Class size ranges from 26 to 36 students, mostly equal in gender split. The following remarks are based on limited exposure after less than six months in the system, and should be read with that in mind. I don't mean to generalize.

Students wear uniforms provided by the school. Some of the smaller children will not fill out their clothes for another year or two. It is not unusual to see a belt wrapped one and a half times around a tiny waist, with a spring clamp securing the belt end somewhere at the back. Students remove their shoes outside the classroom and go around in stocking feet throughout the day, except when changing buildings, going onto the playground, or to the canteen. It is one of the customs that I find extremely tedious—on again, off again with shoes. Teachers, too, remove shoes at the door. I understand this cultural custom and only state my personal aversion.

Janitorial service is practically nil. Students sweep and tidy the buildings for the most part, indoors and out. Even the tiniest pre-schooler can be found sweeping up under lunch tables. Then, of course, students are constantly asked to move furniture to suit an event, and to run errands for teachers.

I haven't counted the number of festivals and religious and state holidays throughout the school year, but they are numerous. Add that to the called-meetings for teachers and extracurricular responsibilities, and the teaching hours are drastically reduced. The sixty-minute class period dwindles, too; by the time a student puts on shoes to change buildings, perhaps stopping at the *hong nahm* before settling back down in the next classroom, he may lose ten minutes. A massive amount of written exercises that should be assigned as homework is done during the class period, further reducing the actual teaching time.

It has been my experience that Thais can't abide quiet time. I am in a co-teaching situation. While I'm trying to present a lesson, my co-teacher will often be reprimanding students (in strident tone) to "sit up", "pay attention", etc. Then she'll proceed to return exercise papers to students or to ask specific questions relating to nothing that is going on in the classroom at the moment, all the while distracting students from the lesson at hand. At times I simply stop teaching altogether until she realizes she is being disruptive. Students are not given enough "think time" or quiet time. They club together and copy from one another habitually, seemingly incapable of completing an assignment independent of friends.

If called upon to answer a question in class, a student looks to his neighbors for an answer. Many simply can't think independently. I was disturbed to discover that listening comprehension is woefully lacking. All told, it becomes very discouraging.

But then there are those two or three students in each class who "get it" with reasonable response time. In my view, the greatest drawback is the lack of spoken English in the classroom. Without question, teachers are competent at teaching reading and writing skills in English, but pitifully few are able to speak English, and thus students are painfully shy, to the point of terror in some cases, afraid to utter a word in English. Not surprisingly.

Teacher shortage has forced school principals to assign English classes to teachers whose major might be in math or science, without even a minor in English. Even those qualified teachers with passable, but often times ungrammatical, English do not speak clearly or distinctly. Students don't have a fighting chance.

I feel that native English speakers like me should be working in teacher training colleges. Until English teachers are better qualified nationwide, I don't think it is reasonable to expect students to learn spoken English at primary and secondary levels without native speakers. I admire those few students who persevere and pursue English in college.

As stated in the beginning, this is one woman's opinion. There is a lot left unwritten between the lines, in deference to my generous and thoughtful hosts.

Bamboo

A small group of us went on an excursion in search of a village where bamboo baskets are made. I couldn't find it again on a bet. We passed through many bamboo groves and twisted and turned down narrow roads and through puddles left by a recent rain. After making a couple of inquiries along the way, we came upon a wizened old gent wearing a broad smile that revealed discolored and missing teeth on his nut-brown furrowed countenance. He turned out to be the village headman. A 'village' seems to consist of a smattering of home sites set back off a dirt road, no visible town or shops and certainly no signs.

We carefully followed his lead on foot down a muddy pathway to a typical two-story Thai-style dwelling. This was the 'factory'. This is where the women in the surrounding area meet whenever they have free time, and they sit and weave baskets. It is reminiscent of the quilting bees of old in America.

These entrepreneurial factories are often under the auspices of OTOP (One Tambon One Product). A tambon is a village community. OTOP is a Thai-government initiative launched in 2001 to promote the sale of unique handmade products made by village communities as a method of income generation at the community level. These tiny villages bring income into the community by choosing their best crop or skill and developing it into a business. In this case, the village nestles among vast bamboo stands. Men and women cut, cure and strip the bamboo. Everyone has a special task. These baskets are very fine, intricate and artistically woven. I can't resist a sizeable purchase. It is a privilege to buy craft items from a person who had a hand in making them.

OTOP assists in the packaging and merchandising. In the case of baskets, no packaging is required. One village might specialize in a particular cookie, others in other food products. OTOP products are handmade, using local materials, traditional wisdom and experience, and techniques handed down from generation to generation. Woven cloth is produced in several areas and each design is distinctive of that area. It is a very good arrangement for the folks in remote villages. It is also a delight to visit these small factories. I have visited weaving factories for silk and cotton cloth, a ceramics workshop and a paper factory that featured beautifully hand-painted umbrellas and other paper products.

In our highly mechanized, over-industrialized and electronic age, it is refreshing to see handmade products being produced with great care and artistry. I fear this may be a dying pastime. We need to appreciate and enjoy these works of art and realize their worth. "Hand Made" may be unknown by future generations.

There are many uses for bamboo in Thailand. I have bought bamboo skewers and toothpicks. Sticky rice is stuffed into foot-long cuts of bamboo and cooked over hot coals—a great favorite of many Thais. Bamboo is a primary building supply used for scaffolding. Furniture is another use; the list goes on. No resource is wasted, but everything is extremely labor intensive.

My Thai family from training days in Ban Pong visited me in Uthai Thani one weekend, to make sure that I was okay. I was pleased to have a supply of beautiful baskets from which to select a gift for my Thai mother (who is 18 years my junior!). It was lovely to see them again.

I will recall a fond memory of the visit to the "bamboo factory" whenever I glance at my baskets in their Aiken home.

Seasonal Changes

The summer heat finally gave way to the occasional overcast day and more-than-welcome rain showers. Daily temperatures now range from 25-35°C (78-95°F). Still hot, but not scorching. Showers sometimes roll gently across the landscape; other times Mother Nature blows up an instant storm and rain pelts down in a rage. Whichever it is to be, I don't dare leave open windows when I set off for school each day. The first big blow caused a power failure that resulted in no water pressure. I was caught without candles or reserve water in the *hong nahm*. I now have a supply of candles handy and a large bucket of reserve water—but have needed neither. We were without power for eight hours that night. I watched a CVD on my computer by battery power, read with a battery-powered book light at bedtime, listened to BBC World Service on my old portable Grundig—and the fridge defrosted itself!

The only thing is, with the seasonal weather change, we have swapped dust, soot and scorching heat for reeking drains covered with deep green scum, puddles that never quite dry up and a slippery, muddy stretch of road in front of my house. Oh, and mosquitoes and a relentless invasion of tiny ants. Thai climate is a lose-lose situation. If I'm not wiping surfaces free of dust and soot, I'm storing stacks of Bangkok Posts beneath each window to absorb the stormy leaks.

Speaking of the Post, I was sitting at the foot of my bed, my back against a plump pillow, reading the Post one day when the tiniest possible spider worked his way down from the ceiling. He would have been invisible from a distance, but he was smack in front of my nose. I had to admire such industry and dexterity. I need to sweep ceilings and corners at least once a month to remove webs.

As I write, I'm observing my new neighbor, male, about 49, polishing his new Toyota—I call it his mistress. I've seen some obsessed new-car owners in my time, but nothing like this guy. We don't visit over the fence, because we don't have a common language. Suits me, because I'm not into small talk. But I swear he'll have the finish worn to bare metal before he puts 10,000 kilometers on the odometer. I felt compelled to give my little city bike its first washing this morning—took about five minutes.

When he first moved in, I could hear every door opening throughout his 'townhouse'—what a misnomer that is. All the hinges squeaked, just as mine did when I first moved in. I soon found a substitute WD-40 and put it to good use. Now, my quandary is how to offer him my spray can so that I can get a full night's sleep in spite of his nocturnal trips to the loo. Over time, I have learned the Thai communication technique of using a third party to make the necessary connections in an awkward situation. "Face" is such an important aspect of Asian culture.

When my cleaning lady/landlady arrived last week, I mimed to her my quandary (much of my life is performed in mime). She took the spray can next door; I heard him chuckle, and the squeaks have disappeared. I have utilized this "third-party" method of communication on several occasions. Some days later, while he was out and away from home, I oiled the rusting gate rollers on his metal security fence.

You may question that I have a "cleaning lady" in a home the size of a shoebox. In this case, it is a matter of staying in touch with my landlady, but more importantly it gives her an added source of income that she needs and which I can afford. Her tasks are few and she takes away my laundry each week, affording her another income source. I could, of course, perform all these tasks myself, with ease.

It probably goes without saying that I also hear every TV program and telephone conversation that goes on next door. Is this what they call 'togetherness'?

So there, you have another glimpse into my world. And as I reach the end of this missile, my neighbor is still out there stroking his mistress.

Internet Travails

The World Wide Web is my link to all things left behind. I wouldn't like to be without it. Email messages from around the world bring a smile, and sometimes a tear, along with news. What a wonderful innovation since the old days of living abroad and waiting weeks, sometimes months, for words from a loved one.

Unfortunately, not all Internet Cafés are created equal. In fact, few are really cafés. They are often cramped storefronts with a dozen out-of-date computers, and software dating to the Dark Ages—which is only a few years back in computerland. Equally unfortunate is the fact that many Internet venues are simply game shops for school kids, with no Internet connection at all.

There is only one bone fide Internet shop in Uthai Thani. It is operated by a young couple and their son. Mum minds the shop, dad goes to work, and son plays on a computer every waking hour. It is situated in their shop house. A shop house is a multi-story building about seventeen feet wide and three stories high. They stand like rigid soldiers, shoulder to shoulder, up and down the streets of Asia.

At ground-level, there is most often a family business. Sometimes there is a shallow mezzanine floor before getting to the second floor and then on up to the third floor, which is often too hot for habitation and is used for storage. In Britain it would be a row house, in America, a townhouse; both on a grander scale than a shop house. Sometimes these ground-level areas are actually the 'front room' for the family. Their whole world passes in review all day long. Many have no solid front wall, just a metal grill that slides to each side, leaving their living room open to the world.

LORETTA J. DUNBAR

But back to my Internet shop—the clangor of kids playing computer games is deafening and the heat is punishing; I'm sitting in sweat. Vertical metal blinds, set flying by an oscillating fan, add to the sound pollution. This was my only option during school holidays. That is, until I made arrangements with a neighbor to bring my laptop to her house and plug into her telephone line. Sounded like a good idea, but, well...

I try to choose times when my neighbor is alone. However on this occasion, shortly after I arrived at her house, someone on a motor cycle pulled up at the gate to visit my hunched-back granny neighbor. Then her grandkids came racing into the front yard, her six-week old Cocker Spaniel puppy chose to poop on the floor near my foot, and rival dogs were tearing at each other in the street. I had just about finished my email messages and was anxious to exit the scene when my cell phone rang. My daughter Mary was calling me from Texas. I quickly logged off, shut down the notebook, disconnected the phone plug and re-connected the neighbor's phone, at the same time trying to carry on a conversation with Mary and get out of there as fast as possible and back to my house two doors away. I stepped carefully over the shit, retrieved the telephone connecting wire, tucked my notebook under one arm, elbowed the door open, phone pressed to my ear, and reached home to conclude the call in relative quiet.

Then classes resumed and I had access to Internet connections at the school, but only for brief periods and not on weekends.

Perhaps I'm seeing a light at the end of the tunnel, for I may be moving to another house where there is a telephone line installed. You might wonder how I ever sent my family thirty essays under the above conditions. I compose on my notebook at home, save it on disk, and when I can access the Internet on a computer with a disk drive, I send the essays to myself by email and hold them in a file until I send them home.

I never paid another visit to use my neighbor's phone connection.

Footnote: since writing this, the only Internet shop in town closed its doors, and I moved into a different house with a telephone hookup.

Housing Upgrade

Life in a shoebox finally got the better of me. A kindly British missionary couple came to my aid just in the nick of time; Bob is English, Jan is Scottish. We met in the local ice cream parlor. I felt an immediate kinship. They are on a one-year temporary re-assignment in a town a couple of hundred kilometers away. They were feeling uneasy about leaving their fully-furnished home here in Uthai Thani unoccupied. They needed a temporary tenant and I needed a change of residence. We struck a deal; I sub-lease. I expect to encounter a whole new set of challenges in a two-story, three-bedroom, and two-bath house, after my simple life in a sweatbox. Hopefully, there will be more plusses than minuses.

There is a small grassy front yard with trees, shrubs and flowering plants, as opposed to the barren cement forecourt at the shoebox. I can sit in the shade on the sheltered front porch and view my orchid plants hanging from the trees. I've engaged a woman to tend to the laundry and house cleaning once a week.

I occupy an upstairs master bedroom, which is about twice the size of my shoebox bedroom, has windows on three sides for light and ventilation, and a built-in air-conditioner. There is a full-size refrigerator, a three-burner gas stove and an old fashioned crockery water filter (made in England), reminiscent of the one I used in Ghana over thirty years ago.

It is an older house, and the plumbing leaves much to be desired. While I had a new Western-style flushing toilet in the shoebox, I now have two toilets that must be flushed by the old fashioned bucket method. I left behind a new water heater in the shoebox and inherited an ancient gas immersion heater here that is just barely functional. The showerheads produced a slow dribble until a friend cleaned out the accumulated corrosion to allow more water flow—then I learned that they will always dribble during the early mornings and late evenings when all the neighbors are trying to shower at once.

I'm fully aware that with all this added real estate I'm probably increasing my potential housekeeping headaches exponentially. Can't win for losing. But I do enjoy relaxing in a proper living room chair instead at the foot of my bed, as I have done for over six months. I also enjoy sitting on the porch in the morning with the Bangkok Post, along with my breakfast tray. I take most of my meals out there. It is not a patch on my cozy home in South Carolina, but it is a major upgrade in Uthai Thani.

There is a telephone connection that allows me access to the Internet. The bicycling distance to my two schools is about the same, maybe a tad shorter. I can even be out by bicycle after dark, after being confined at night for five months. The red dirt road had become impassable in the rainy season.

I'm now getting acquainted with my new neighborhood and establishing routes to schools and shops. I've moved from the far north of town to the far south; more convenient to some things and less convenient to others.

I still have yapping dogs right next door and the 6 a.m. public address system still persists, as do all the other neighborhood sounds. But at least I have a little more breathing space—if only a few feet. The house has accumulated years of grime as a result of neglect and loose housekeeping standards. I must go through ritual padlocking of gates, grilled security doors, etc, each time I leave the house—a great nuisance. But still I'm more comfortable. I've used a lot of elbow grease to make my nesting area more suitable to my standard, but the house is packed with family possessions that include nine bookcases stuffed with paperbacks—religious for the most part, reference books, and only a few books on the lighter side, all enveloped in years of accumulated dust.

THAI ODYSSEY

Bob and Jan retain the privilege of keeping one of the bedrooms for their personal use whenever they need to be back in town. Works for me.

The garden had become very overgrown, so I engaged a man to clean up a bit. He had nearly scalped the place before I got out to say *nit noi*—only a little! I'm afraid Bob and Jan may have a shock on their first visit, but it will grow back soon enough.

I looked like a real "Okie" on moving day. My worldly possessions were packed higgledy-piggledy on the back of Bob's 30-year-old Suzuki pick-up truck for two round trips. His second car is an equally ancient, bright red Mazda sports car held together by a coat of paint and God's will. These good folks have lived out here their entire married life and raised five children along the way. I admire them tremendously.

The climate remains my nemesis even though more tolerable in my new surroundings. I am often able to forego air-conditioning during this rainy season, but am thankful it is there when I need it.

And the Beat Goes On

I recently had cause to be in Bangkok over a weekend following a two-week workshop with Peace Corps at Cha-Am beach resort area, and prior to a dental appointment on the Monday morning. I had done a little research during an earlier visit to Bangkok and located a small hotel centrally placed and convenient to public transportation. Sam's Lodge has only twenty rooms and they are on the three stories above his tailoring business at ground level. It is two adjoining shop houses fused together, so of course is very narrow. Many rooms have no windows. There is no space for baths in the rooms, so showers, toilets and wash basins are located at the end of the hall. It is clean, convenient and reasonably priced.

I decided to devote time to learning my way around the city on public transportation and to overdose on luxuries (excluding accommodation!). I arrived in Bangkok at mid-afternoon on Saturday. My first stop was a nearby department store and straight to the food market, where I selected some ground beef and bacon and asked the butcher to freeze it for me and I would pick it up before noon on Monday. He was very accommodating. Then I walked a block to the nearest Sky Train station and bought a Sky Card for 200 baht that allows me easy entry and exit to the trains until it runs out. My next stop was the Emporium Cineplex. I bought popcorn and enjoyed viewing Spiderman Two in air-conditioned comfort.

After the movie, I ate at a restaurant in the Emporium department store and headed back to Sam's Lodge, where I spent the evening planning my schedule for Sunday. I had read an ad in the Bangkok Post for a Mexican restaurant at a posh hotel about one kilometer from

Sam's. I also wanted to try out the newly opened subway system and the river taxi.

Here is my day: I left the lodge at 9:30 Sunday morning and took the Sky Train to an exchange point for the subway. I found it without too much difficulty, having poured over city maps at length. I took the subway to the next exchange point, disembarked and got back on the Sky Train to take me to Central Pier to catch a river taxi up the Chao Phra Ya River. I disembarked at the Grand Palace, took a quick walk in front of the Palace and got back on the river taxi and reversed my route. All this before noon, when I planned to see the newest Harry Potter film—once again at the Emporium. After the movie, I briefly met with some Thai friends at Siam Center and continued shopping before returning to Sam's.

Yes, I was tired. The Sky Train is a great way to get around, but it involves a lot of tramping up and down stairs at access points and bridge crossings over the teeming, noisy roadways below. Bangkok is not a fun place. The subway is clean and spacious, but there is no signage in English. Tourists will need to know their stops ahead of time. It is reminiscent of the London subway, but without any advertising on the escalator walls. A good map showing both Sky Train route and the Subway route is available at Sky Train stations. Public transportation is not for weaklings; one must walk, walk, and walk.

I had done the tourist thing years earlier and visited all the primary sites, so was not interested in a repeat. I've seen enough temples to last me a lifetime. I just wanted to know my way around for those quick shopping trips to Bangkok from time to time.

On Sunday night I headed for the Rembrandt Hotel and some Mexican fare. It turned out to be a longer walk than I wanted, and next time I'll do it by taxi. I was lucky to be seated without a reservation, for no sooner had I arrived when the place began to fill up with large parties, mostly expatriates. I ordered nachos. They weren't like any nachos I have ever had before, but the ingredients were not bad and

THAI ODYSSEY

I enjoyed my meal. Unfortunately, there wasn't a taxi handy when I started back to the hotel, so it was another long walk.

I was back on the Sky Train early Monday for my dental appointment. Here again, the calculated distance from the Sky Train station to the hospital was too long a walk; live and learn. Next time, a taxi. Never have I had such vigorous cleaning of my teeth. Great facility, quick and efficient; but I didn't look forward to a repeat visit. Then it was back by taxi (I'm learning!) to Sam's; run over to pick up the frozen meat and add some cheese and salami; check out of the lodge; taxi to the van station and—whoa! Let me out of here!

I swear that taxi driver had a death wish and me with it. Believe it; I was shouting at him to slow down, pull over, let me out (we were on a multi-lane expressway and no way out)—he was adamant. I believed he was taking me the long way, he swore otherwise. Yeah, even with the best preplanning in the world, you can still get screwed. I did make it to the van station (a nervous, angry wreck) for the three-hour van ride home to Uthai Thani before dark.

I want a long breather before I make another visit to the city.

A Visit to Chiang Mai

Everyone who visits Thailand wants to see Chiang Mai, 700km north of Bangkok. The climate is slightly more comfortable at 1,000 feet above sea level; not any cooler, but a little less humid. It sits in a valley surrounded by low hills covered in lush vegetation. I'm told there are lovely resorts in the outlying areas, where a wood-burning fire is a comfort on cool winter evenings.

I traveled to Chiang Mai by comfortable air-conditioned direct VIP bus. The 500km journey back to Uthai Thani would take a full 9-5 work day and three modes of transportation. More about that later.

Chiang Mai was too big for me (250,000 population); too much like Bangkok with respect to heavy traffic, pollution, and overload of tourists and tour buses. On the plus side, *songtaos* will take you anywhere, much like a taxi service, and are inexpensive. Of course, the catch is that you must be able to name the place you're going to, and remember how to get back to your hotel.

Hotels look good outside, but are still the same standard I've encountered in other Thai cities: poorly finished construction, soiled inferior-grade carpets, out-of-date plumbing fixtures, skimpy toiletries, low maintenance standards, no coffee/tea supplies in the rooms, etc, unless you frequent five-star venues—where you'll get what you pay for. My allowance keeps me in the lower ranks.

A local friend took me to the night bazaar, a shopper's paradise. The one in Chiang Mai is large, requiring plenty of walking. I saw some lovely handcrafts and bought two gauzy cotton scarves from one of the tiniest ladies I've ever met, probably a size zero or smaller, perfectly proportioned and wearing a charming smile. When I paid for my purchase, she took the 100 baht note and walked around the shop touching all the remaining shelves of goods in her display. I was her first customer of the evening and this ritual is meant to bring her good luck and good sales for the remainder of the evening. It is of Chinese origin and I had seen it done in an earlier visit to Asia.

Much is made of façades. There is abundant use of ceramic tile, gold paint and ornamentation in hotels, temples and even in private homes, but internal spaces don't live up to expectations, mostly due to poor craftsmanship, poor maintenance and lack of originality. Electrical installations and outlets are particularly poor and scarce. Thermostats are often functionless; either on or off, no real temperature regulation. Sometimes installations are backwards— 'high' is low, 'hot' is cold, etc. These conditions apply to the older buildings. However, many city hotels are up-market—where you pay Western prices.

As in some European hotels, the plastic key card activates the electrical supply when slipped into a slot just inside your hotel room. This is a reasonable power- and cost-saving solution. As you leave the room you retrieve the key card and there is a brief delay before all electrical supply shuts down, including air-conditioning.

There are graduated levels of transportation possibilities in Thailand. I traveled to and from Chiang Mai on three classes of bus: VIP, first-class and cheap, non-air-conditioned varieties, as well as *songtao* and motorized tuk-tuk. A motorized tuk-tuk is a rickshaw powered by a motorcycle engine. Some rickshaws are powered by push bike. On a visit to Asia in the late 1980s I rode in my first rickshaw pulled by a person on foot. I don't think those exist today except perhaps in remote Asian villages.

The lesson I learned was—always travel long-distance by VIP bus where available. These are especially good for overnight journeys. The seats recline similar to airline business-class seats. The toilet was reasonable in the back of the bus and snacks were passable. On the other hand, the *hong nahm* in the first-class bus was unbelievable. It was on the lower level of the bus. There was a large plastic water-filled barrel and dipper that occupied 90% of the airline-sized cubicle. It needed a contortionist to accomplish the mission intended. If you came away without wet garments, you were very clever indeed. Obviously, the floor was continuously wet and slippery. The quality of the food snacks was on a par with the *hong nahm*. Needless to say from there on down the transportation ladder you are roughing it.

My visit to Chiang Mai was a good trip for information gathering. I learned that if you see something you want and you haven't seen it before, especially with craft items, buy it on the spot. Chances are that it is regional and you might not see it again along your travels. I bought woven cotton rugs in Nan and cotton scarves and paper products in Chiang Mai. I usually buy blank note cards during my worldwide travels to use for greeting cards. Often times they are handmade and a nice change from our beautiful Hallmark cards at six times the price.

On the bright side: people were helpful all along the way. When language failed me, friendly Thais did their best to point me to my next destination, and some used English language.

Food and drink offerings deteriorated with the level of service. The non-air local bus for a 45km segment near the end of my journey was the most uncomfortable. It was beastly hot in the plains area; curtains flapping at the windows, oscillating overhead fans pushing hot air around, and frequent stops for departing passengers.

General impression: It is impossible to learn or understand a culture while on a tourist visit. I am privileged to be able to live in the circumstances I have described through many essays and to begin to have a little insight into life in the world of Asia.

Thai Mother's Day

Each year on August 12, Her Majesty Queen Sirikit's birthday is celebrated as a national holiday and as Thailand's Mother's Day. This year she celebrates her 72nd or 6th cycle birthday. In Thailand, "cycle" birthdays—periods of 12 years—are most notable of all.

The Queen is renowned for her good works during her fifty-four years of service. As one would expect from a queen, she has been active in every facet of the kingdom, revitalizing interest and promoting everything Thai.

There is some serious nationwide celebrating this year throughout the land. Preparations began months in advance. Each Friday, for the entire year, many people wear a sky-blue knit shirt with the Queen's crest emblazoned thereon, in recognition of this special birthday. These shirts are worn weekly right through the end of the calendar year.

During the week of the official Mother's Day, I joined my colleagues and a community women's group for a visit to the female section of the local prison. We took gift parcels from the Queen to distribute to the inmates, each containing a ceramic mug, hand soap, washcloth, toothbrush and toothpaste. Most of the young women were convicted on drug trafficking. We served them their noon meal after presenting them with the gifts.

We had an opportunity to observe their living conditions. It was frightening—enough to make me think twice before risking that kind of confinement. The cell walls are of cement blocks waist high, with metal mesh from there on up to the ceiling. Several inmates share each enclosure—dorm style. There are raised wooden platforms taking up most of the cell space. The women sleep on these platforms with only a blanket. It is an open-air cage with a ceiling fan; no chair, table, anything—only the sleeping platform. The latrines are simply waist-high concrete separation walls at the back of the cell. You are visible from the waist up. There is not an inch of privacy. Each woman has a personal locker half the size of a high school book locker along the low walls outside of the cells.

What really struck me is how they could tolerate the extreme heat of this climate in those conditions. They wear simple smock-like cotton tops and trousers of a pleasant shade of blue. Male inmates wear similar garments in pink. Go figure.

The open-air dining area is adjacent to the cells—simple tables and benches. It is a compact and confining area altogether. I am 100% miserable in this climate at the best of times; how must it be for these poor women.

The day before Mother's Day, the school children gathered as usual in the school quadrangle and a serious, two-hour ceremony took place to honor the Queen. There was a life-size portrait of the Queen placed in center stage, festooned with garlands and flowers. It was as if she were there in the flesh. Students performed Thai dances, songs were sung and speeches given; loyal followers bowed and curtsied in front of the portrait as if it were a living being.

Then a truckload of monks arrived to receive gifts of rice and packaged snack foods as well as soft drinks and water, all donated by the students. The food was placed on long tables in the yard. The monks paraded in front of the tables and students and teachers placed food and beverages in their begging bowls, which in turn were dumped into large baskets held by male students walking behind the monks, and carted off to the canteen tables for separation into equalized small gift packets packaged in plastic bags and sealed with rubber bands. These small packets were, in turn, taken to a local hospital and given to the patients—all this in honor of the Queen.

I, my colleagues and a handful of representative students drove to the hospital, followed by a pick-up truck loaded with the gift parcels. We walked through the wards of each building, distributing largess to patients.

The following evening, August 12, a co-teacher picked me up to attend the final celebration of dancing and merrymaking at the local sports stadium, topped off with a real July Fourth-like fireworks display.

The disturbing part of all this, to me, is that I taught only about 10 class hours all through the month of August. Classes were frequently cancelled due to meetings in connection with Mother's Day plans and activities. Students were often excused from class to go to practice for one thing or another. Teachers had many extracurricular duties connected to the holiday. Even when I did co-conduct classes, students were usually making Mother's Day cards or other fun activities, but not necessarily studying.

More than that, the school Sport Day was scheduled for the week following Mother's Day, so students were practicing for competition for weeks in advance. From my perspective, the entire month of August was a write off with regard to classroom lessons. I was told that conditions would revert to normal in September, and they did.

Thais are renowned for their smiles and their propensity for *sanook*—fun—but at what cost to education?

Epilogue

My essays came to an abrupt end in August 2004. September was a time of final exams for the students and there were few "new" experiences happening. After all, I had been in the country since January.

In the beginning, I had no concerns about the tropical weather that I was to encounter in Thailand, because I had spent a total of eight years in West Africa: four years in Ghana, followed by four years in Nigeria. I thought I was quite acclimated to the tropics. But none of those years compares with the intensity of the heat in Thailand. I began losing hair at an alarming rate and other minor medical concerns developed.

Early on, while still in the training phase, I stubbed both of my big toes at various times while pedaling a bicycle. In a culture where sandals are the norm and feet have little or no protection, it was inevitable. Those injuries were slow to heal, and while they didn't interfere with my work, I was in pain throughout my time in Thailand and long after returning home.

When the end of the school term approached in September, I did some hard soul searching. When I accepted the assignment eighteen months earlier, I understood that I would be teaching Thai teachers to teach English. That made sense. The Thai government was anxious to promote spoken English in the schools. However, soon after beginning my assignment, it became clear that very few Thai English teachers could speak the language. They did a fine job of teaching grammar, and often times the students could read quite well, but comprehension lagged too much; local teachers were teaching

English in Thai language. It just doesn't work. Students were petrified of opening their mouths to utter something in English for fear of poor pronunciation.

By the time this became apparent, I was firmly entrenched into the system, having been through three months of training and moved onto my teaching site. I was assigned to teach classes in just two levels, approximately seventh and eighth graders. That assignment was made because the only Thai English teacher who could actually speak reasonable English was teaching at those levels. Therefore, Jiripa was assigned to me and me to her, as co-teachers. Jiripa was my savior, my interpreter, and became my very dear friend.

I was assigned to serve two schools. At the second school, Kuhn Tim spoke broken English and was less secure with it. By the way, the word "Kuhn" is equivalent to Miss or Mrs. and that polite title is used with first names during working hours. I was known as Kuhn Etta, as explained in one of the essays.

Kuhn Tim (female, despite the name) was generous, gracious and supportive in every way. She hosted my initial visit to Uthai Thani and while I expected her to be my primary liaison in the community, it was Kuhn Jiripa with whom I spent most of my time.

One day, some parents of twelfth graders approached a principal and demanded that their children have lessons with me, because they were about to enter university and would not have another opportunity to learn from a native English speaker. Class hours were already assigned and full, but I suggested that if we could combine those upper level classes in one large classroom at least once a week, I would work with them. In addition to this, I organized an evening English class for teachers, parents and local citizens at large. Granted, such large classes are rarely effective in the teaching of a foreign language, but it was a band-aid approach that satisfied most people. There was a tremendous desire to learn English language, but little or no time for class work or study in the very busy lives of teachers in Thailand.

THAI ODYSSEY

Some parents urged me to do private tutoring of their young children. This is prohibited by Peace Corps, for they well know that volunteers ultimately get burned out if they take on too much extra teaching. Nevertheless, I did, for a short time, have a couple of young students come to my house after school once a week.

Because there were so many demands on my time, I was spread terribly thin. No progress was being made. Some classes saw me only once a week for a 50-minute period. With 36 students in each class, this simply wasn't enough time for them to receive and absorb language instruction.

In August, near the end of the term, I began contemplating a vacation in a cooler climate during the summer school break. I decided that New Zealand was the nearest cool climate in the month of October, and planned accordingly. During that holiday, I really thought long and hard about the prospect of spending another year and a half in the same circumstances, with the same medical concerns and the same lack of progress in the teaching situation. I knew that I had to make a decision by the time I returned to Thailand and before the next school term began.

Peace Corps has very stringent regulations about leaving the Corps. They unquestioningly accept any reason whatsoever, and never try to change your mind. But when you tell the office of your decision, you are out of the country within 24 to 48 hours. During that time you must go through an extensive final medical and physical examination, pack up all your gear and say your goodbyes—because you'll be on the next plane home. Also, you may not stay in the country and take a vacation before leaving the country. Peace Corps pays your fare home and you leave immediately. I know there are several reasons for these regulations, that needn't be listed here.

With that knowledge, I had taken the precaution of packing many of my meager possessions before leaving for New Zealand, but still hoping I might rekindle the desire to remain to the end of my tour.

Ultimately I decided I had more to lose and less to gain by staying. I believed that I could return to my volunteer teaching position in the United States and achieve more than I was in Thailand, and could address my health issues at home as well.

It was with tremendous self-disappointment that I walked into the Peace Corps office in Bangkok in late November and asked to terminate my contract. Bangkok is 235 miles south of my home in Uthai Thani. The office assigned a staff driver to take me to my home by van. He was instructed to wait while I packed my belongings, arranged for all loose ends to be taken care of, i.e. utility bills, telling my landlord of my immediate departure, disposing of those things I wouldn't bring home, spend an overnight, and then to bring me back to Bangkok the next day. I barely had a chance to say goodbye to my co-teachers and the directors, before I was whisked back to Bangkok. They had set up a series of medical appointments for me to meet throughout the following day in Bangkok, before handing me my plane ticket home. I knew the drill.

Despite that expeditious exit, I look back and cherish the experiences with the Thai people. The teaching experience was a disappointment, but time spent with one of the most welcoming and generous people I've ever met, remains precious to me.

The rest of the story is that I did indeed return to teaching English as a Second Language in my home town for a couple more years. When I decided to discontinue classroom teaching altogether, another door opened for me and I began private tutoring of English as a Second Language. This has proven to be the ultimate teaching challenge and reward.

You may ask what possessed me to join the Peace Corps in the first instance in 1971. I was probably entering a mid-life crisis and wanted to see what the rest of the world was doing. I was married to a physician, had a lovely home and all that goes with it. My only child, Mary, was in college. I guess I didn't particularly feel needed at the time. Besides, I had married young and now wanted to do all the things I had put aside at that time in order to support my pre-med husband and infant daughter.

I was approaching forty when I contemplated Peace Corps service. In those days, I felt that if I were ever going to cut loose and see the world it had better be done before I got too old. That's a bit of a laugh, because I still have as much energy and zest for adventure, at the age of seventy-five, as I did at forty. I've sailed around the world and then some, visited more than sixty countries, and still going.

My message to you is, if you have a dream, don't wait to pursue it.

LJD